THAT GOOD BETWEEN US

Credentials of a Sympathizer

By the same author

Stage Plays

Cheek
No One Was Saved
Alpha Alpha
Edward, the Final Days
Stripwell
Claw
Fair Slaughter
The Love of a Good Man
The Hang of the Gaol
The Loud Boy's Life

T.V. Plays

Cows
Mutinies
Prowling Offensive
Conrod
Heroes of Labour
Russia
All Bleeding
Heaven

Radio Plays

One Afternoon on the 63rd Level of the North Face
of the Pyramid of Cheops the Great
Henry V in Two Parts
Herman with Millie and Mick

PLAYSCRIPT 92

THAT GOOD BETWEEN US
Credentials of a Sympathizer

Howard Barker

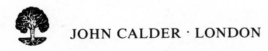

JOHN CALDER · LONDON

First published in Great Britain, 1980, by
John Calder (Publishers) Ltd.,
18 Brewer Street, London W1R 4AS

That Good Between Us originally published 1977
by John Calder (Publishers) Ltd. in *Gambit 31*

All performing rights in these plays are strictly reserved and
applications for performance should be made to:
Judy Daish Associates Ltd.,
Globe Theatre,
Shaftesbury Avenue,
London W1A 7AA

No performance of these plays may be given unless a licence has
been obtained prior to rehearsal.

British Library Cataloguing in Publication Data
Barker, Howard
    That good between us (Playscript 92)
    I. Title II. Series
    822'.9' 14   PR6052.A6485T/

ISBN 0 7145 3799 3 Hardback
ISBN 0 7145 3765 9 Paperback

Typeset in 9/10 pt Press Roman by Gilbert Compsing Services Ltd.,
    Leighton Buzzard.
Printed by M. & A. Thomson Litho Ltd., East Kilbride
Bound by Hunter & Foulis Ltd., Edinburgh

CONTENTS

To My Mother and Father

That Good Between Us

Wandering between two worlds, one dead,
The other powerless to be born.
Matthew Arnold

That Good Between Us was first performed at the RSC's Warehouse Theatre in Covent Garden, July 28th, 1977.

The cast were:

MCPHEE	Ian McDiarmid
GODBER	John Nettles
KNATCHBULL	Patrick Stewart
BLEACH	David Lyon
ORBISON	Barbara Leigh-Hunt
RHODA	Cherie Lunghi
VERITY	Sarah Eyton
MAJOR CADBURY	Hubert Rees
CORPORAL TELLING	David Howey
PRIVATE EDEN/CYCLIST/POLICEMAN	Rod Culbertson
PRIVATE HART/JUMBO/RIOT SOLDIER	Alfred Molina
PRIVATE RICE/ABJABS/CYCLIST	Christopher Whitehouse
PRIVATE HAYMAN/HIS CORPSE/ SECOND COUNCIL EMPLOYEE/ MILITARY POLICEMAN	Kevin O'Shea
MURPHY	Clyde Pollitt
NADINE	Judith Harte
SIMONE/WOMAN IN CAR	Judy Monahan
CABBAGE THROWER/MILITARY POLICEMAN/MAN WITH BROOM/ FIRST COUNCIL EMPLOYEE	Martin Read
CLERGYMAN/MAN IN CAR/ RIOT SOLDIER	Paul Wagar

Directed by Barry Kyle

ACT ONE

Scene One

A dark night at sea somewhere off the Devon coast. A distant lighthouse flashes at five second intervals. From some distance, a voice with a strong Glasgow accent singing badly 'Everybody needs Somebody' by the Rolling Stones. The voice grows louder, comes nearer. A rowing boat appears stage left, containing three men. Two of them, the oarsman BLEACH, and KNATCHBULL, wear overcoats and are seated. The third, MCPHEE, is standing and wears only a thin shirt and trousers. His is the singing voice. About the centre of the stage, BLEACH stops rowing, looks to KNATCHBULL.

BLEACH. How's this? What's wrong with this?

KNATCHBULL *(to MCPHEE)*. Billy, if you don't mind. . .

BLEACH. Have mercy, Billy.

MCPHEE *(seizing on another Rolling Stones number)*. 'Have mer—cy, Have mer—cy, ba—by. . .'

KNATCHBULL. All right! Can't fucking think straight! *(The singing stops.)* Thank you. (KNATCHBULL *stands up carefully, looks around.)*

MCPHEE. Is this it, then?

KNATCHBULL. I think so. I think so, yes.

BLEACH. This spot is as good as any. I would say.

MCPHEE. I'm easy.

KNATCHBULL. He's not choosey.

BLEACH. He's no trouble, are you, son?

MCPHEE. I'm nae trouble. Not to noobody.

KNATCHBULL. That's the ticket.

MCPHEE. What aboot the lighthouse?

KNATCHBULL. They won't see nothing.

MCPHEE. Just wonderin'. . .

KNATCHBULL. No, they won't see buggerall.

BLEACH. It's a good five miles away.

MCPHEE. Funny thing, I was over there today. . .

BLEACH. Go on.

MCPHEE. It's free. A nice smart geezer shows yoo round. They ha' these soddin' great big lenses, you knoo. Bloody big they are. An' this geezer has to clean 'em, wi' a chamois, every day.

3

BLEACH.　Fuck that.
MCPHEE.　That's what I said.
BLEACH.　Fuckin' drag.
MCPHEE.　An' the whole lot is floatin' on a bed of mercury.
BLEACH.　Is that so?
MCPHEE.　A ton of mercury.
BLEACH.　Well, well.
MCPHEE.　I was knocked oot. An' they let yoo look at it. For nothin'. I was knocked oot.
BLEACH.　That's very wonderful.
MCPHEE.　As a token of my appreciation I made a donation to the lifeboats.
BLEACH.　That's only fair.
MCPHEE.　Yeah, well they're good people, aren't they?
BLEACH.　That's right. They are.

Long pause. The boat is still.

KNATCHBULL.　Billy, before we get down to business, I'd like to say a special thank you. From Mr. Bleach here and myself.
BLEACH.　Yup.

Pause.

MCPHEE.　What for?
KNATCHBULL.　For going about this so intelligently. For making the minimum of fuss. We do appreciate it.
BLEACH.　Yup. Sincerely.
KNATCHBULL.　We mean that. *(Pause. They look at him.)* Now, take your things off, Billy, please. Like you were going for a swim.
BLEACH.　Down to your pants. (MCPHEE *doesn't move. Pause.)* If you would, please. (MCPHEE *still doesn't move.)*
KNATCHBULL.　We've got a long row back, lad. *(Pause, then he yells.)* Come on, lad! (MCPHEE *remains motionless.* KNATCHBULL *stands up, balancing carefully.)*
BLEACH.　Mind how you stand up, Ronald—
KNATCHBULL.　Come on, lad!
BLEACH *(leaning to balance the boat).*　Have us over—
KNATCHBULL *(to* BLEACH).　All right!

Pause. MCPHEE *looks at them, then suddenly bursts into song.*

MCPHEE.　'This could be the last time, This could be the last time, it may be the last time, I don't know, No, no, No, no. . .'
KNATCHBULL.　Don't blot your copybook.
MCPHEE.　Jagger-Richards.
KNATCHBULL.　Don't fuck it up.

Pause.

MCPHEE. Yoo are a pair of bastards. That's what yoo are.

BLEACH. We will be in a minute. We'll be right bastards in a minute.

MCPHEE. Yoo'll go to hell, the pair of yoo!

KNATCHBULL. Don't start all that.

MCPHEE. I'm tellin' yoo yoo will! Yoo'll suffer for eternity!

BLEACH. Oh dear, oh dear. . .

MCPHEE. Wicked torment for terrible men!

KNATCHBULL. Undress! *(Pause, then* MCPHEE *begins to unbutton his shirt.)* Thank you. Thank you very much indeed.

MCPHEE *unzips his trousers, lets them fall.*

BLEACH. Wind blowing up. *(Keeping his balance,* MCPHEE *steps out of his trousers, then removing his shirt, drops it into the bottom of the boat. He is naked but for his pants.* BLEACH *looks at him.)* All things considered, you should have stuck to buggery. . .

MCPHEE. What if I make it? I've done a mile. I've got the fuckin' certificate to prove it! What happens if I make it, eh?

KNATCHBULL. We will look berks.

MCPHEE. Yoo fuckin' will!

KNATCHBULL. But you won't. I wouldn't entertain false hopes.

MCPHEE. I'll fuckin' try!

KNATCHBULL. Of course you'll try.

BLEACH. Be bloody stupid if you didn't try.

KNATCHBULL. Even with this current, you're bound to try.

MCPHEE. I'll goo with it. Tread water. Let it carry me.

KNATCHBULL. Into the Atlantic?

MCPHEE. Meet a ship!

KNATCHBULL. In the dead of night?

BLEACH. Rocks more likely.

MCPHEE. All right, then, rocks!

KNATCHBULL. Head first. I would have thought. . . (MCPHEE *looks from one to the other. Pause.)* Ta ta, Billy.

Pause, then MCPHEE *sits on the gunwale. He looks at them, then gingerly dips a foot in the water.*

MCPHEE. Christ! *(He grins uneasily.)* It's cold. . .

BLEACH. I bet.

MCPHEE *hesitates, looks back appealingly.*

KNATCHBULL. Bye bye, we said.

MCPHEE *slides into the water with a shiver.*

MCPHEE. Ohhhhh. . .

BLEACH. Try doing the butterfly.

MCPHEE *shudders again, his hand still on the gunwale. At last he lets go.* KNATCHBULL *bends, picks up an oar and hands it to* BLEACH. BLEACH *stands, raises the oar fully above his head.*

MCPHEE. Hey! Tha's nae fair! (BLEACH *brings the oar down with all his strength.)* Jesus Christ! Tha's nae fuckin' fair! (BLEACH *strikes again.)* Gi' us a chance! *(As* BLEACH *rains down blows,* KNATCHBULL *leans this way and that to maintain an even keel.)* Yoo fuckin' cheat! (BLEACH *leans further out to strike.)* Oh, help me, Christ! Save me! *(The last blow lands.* BLEACH *regains his balance, then sits, wearily, head in hands.)*

KNATCHBULL *(looking at the current).* Away he goes. . . *(Pause.)* Dump his clothing on the beach. And then scoot off. All right? (BLEACH *doesn't move.)* All right? (BLEACH *still doesn't react.* KNATCHBULL *sits, rubs his face.)* Oh, dear . . . *(Pause.)* Oh, dear, oh, dear. . . *(Pause.)* What is it now?

BLEACH *(resentfully).* My bloody arm. All that. Ricked my bloody arm.

Blackout on the boat.

Scene Two

A street in London. Three SOLDIERS *in work fatigues appear from different areas of the stage, dragging or carrying dustbins. They upturn them, sit on them wearily. At that moment, a man rushes on and throws a rotting cabbage. One of the soldiers parries with a dustbin lid.*

MAN. Forgot somethin', you army bastards! *(He runs off again as two* RIOT SOLDIERS, *in battle kit, charge after him, yelling and wielding clubs. The three sit again, one rolls a cigarette.)*

RICE. In China—

EDEN. Fuck China.

RICE. In China the upper classes do this sort of thing.

TELLING. There are no upper classes in China. They have eradicated 'em. They have stuffed 'em down the lavatory and pulled the chain.

RICE. The geezers with the money, then.

TELLING. They don't have geezers with money.

RICE. Fucking hell, you know what I mean! Surgeons empty shit-pans, that's what I mean.

Pause, then the MAN *appears at the opposite side of the stage. This time he flings a plastic bag full of peelings at them.*

MAN. Forgot somethin', you army bastards!

The men duck, the MAN *rushes off, followed by the yelling, club-wielding* RIOT SOLDIERS. *Pause.*

EDEN *(recalling with difficulty).*   China—is—the—sher—bert—
foun—tain—of—the—intell—ectuals. . .
TELLING.   I am sick of China.
EDEN.   I never brought it up.
TELLING.   Fucking China. All we ever hear about is China!
EDEN.   The Major. His words.
TELLING.   Shut up.
EDEN.   I quote the Major. Let me quote the Major.
TELLING.   SHUT UP.
RICE.   Here he comes! *(They all slide off their bins and duck as
the* MAN *reappears, holding a bag of rotting fruit. Only this
time he isn't able to throw it or speak, as the* RIOT SOLDIERS
*are too close behind him. He stops. Then rushes out again. The
men get back on their bins.)* This time last week we were stoking
ovens in Doncaster.
EDEN.   The week before that shunting goods wagons in Burnley.
RICE.   I enjoyed that. *(Pause. The other two look at him.)* I did.
I enjoyed it.
TELLING.   I have had enough of it! I have had a gutful of strike-
breaking! Next week we're protecting blacklegs in Portsmouth.
EDEN.   Patience, Col. . .
TELLING.   Fuck patience.
EDEN.   Patience—is—the—secret—weapon—of—the—masses.
TELLING.   You and your fucking quotations. We have an
organization. We have a set-up. And we are doing nothing!
(He shuts up as the two RIOT SOLDIERS *swagger in.)*
1st RIOT SOLDIER.   We will do him. We will de-bollock him.
2nd RIOT SOLDIER.   No more little communists.
TELLING.   Yeah. Do him.

*Pause. A Major enters, portly and slovenly. He is accompanied by a
wireless operator. The men slide off their bins.*

CADBURY.   All right. All right.

Suddenly, the MAN *reappears. He stands, waiting for them to notice
him. All the soldiers turn.*

MAN.   You're attacking us! You are workers and you're attacking
us!

*He hesitates as if expecting a response. Then, out of the silence
comes a low growl, deep in the throats of the* RIOT SOLDIERS
*holding the clubs. It builds up into a yell, until they launch
themselves like missiles at the* MAN, *who flees.* TELLING *kicks
his bin angrily.*

TELLING.   What are we doing! What are we DOING!

CADBURY *(introducing the wireless operator).* This is
     Hayman. Hayman is a comrade.
RICE. Mick Hayman, ain't it?
HAYMAN. S'right.
PRICE. Welcome, Comrade.
CADBURY. Hayman is our contact in the Signals.
HAYMAN. This is something. This is really something, ain't it?
CADBURY. We are very small yet. What we are learning is the
     art of patience.
EDEN. 'Patience is the secret weapon of the masses.'
TELLING. That's right. We're chock full of patience. We have
     it with our breakfast.

The two RIOT SOLDIERS *appear, dragging the* MAN *between
them. They force him to the ground in front of* CADBURY.

1ST RIOT SOLDIER. One commie bastard, sir.
2ND RIOT SOLDIER. Say somethin'!
1ST RIOT SOLDIER. Not so chatty.
2ND RIOT SOLDIER. Say somethin'!

The MAN *refuses to speak.* CADBURY *looks at him.*

CADBURY. You communists. You are ruining Britain. Do you
     know that?

The two RIOT SOLDIERS *look at one another.*

2ND RIOT SOLDIER *(thrusting him forward).* ANS—WER!
CADBURY. Go home and stay indoors. If you are apprehended
     again, it will go badly for you. Do you understand that?
2ND RIOT SOLDIER. ANS—WER!

CADBURY *indicates they should take him away. The two* RIOT
SOLDIERS *are amazed, but begin leading him away.* TELLING
rushes up and kicks the MAN *viciously in the back. The* MAN *yells,
and the* RIOT SOLDIERS *run off with him.* TELLING *comes back.*

RICE. You hurt him. You hurt him.
TELLING. You saw what they were thinking.
RICE. You fucking hurt him.
TELLING. Someone had to do something! *(He is looking critically
     at* CADBURY.) Christ, if we are discovered, CHRIST!
CADBURY. Colin's right. We can't be squeamish. Sometimes we
     must outdo them. The revolution calls on your malice, and your
     violence, as well as your hope. It will be a haemmhoraging of
     your hopes, a dysentry of your good will. Only the best of you
     will keep faith. Remember that.
TELLING *(shouldering his bin).* You heard the Major! Come on!

They pick up their bins, disperse to work. Blackout.

Scene Three

*A sunny day on the Serpentine. Midstage a rowing boat containing
two women, ORBISON, in her late forties, at the oars, and RHODA,
her daughter lounging in the stern. An atmosphere of heat and tension,
and a long pause.*

ORBISON: I am missing a cabinet meeting to be here!
RHODA. That's what they call living dangerously.
ORBISON. Why do we have to meet here? Why the bloody Serpentine?
RHODA. I loathe restaurants.
ORBISON. What about me?
RHODA. You will have to learn to survive outside restaurants. The
air is thin, but there is life.
ORBISON. I hate water.
RHODA. No. You are terrified of being shot.
ORBISON. I have always hated water. I never took you in the water
as a child. Surely you remember that.
RHODA. You are terrified someone will pick you off.
ORBISON. Will you stop.
RHODA. Home Secretary zapped on Serpentine.
ORBISON. Please!
RHODA. You're sweating.
ORBISON. I am hot.
RHODA. When I was a kid you were always prancing round the
supermarkets sucking up to housewives. Now every shopping
basket hides a bomb. You are all terrified. You are under siege.
ORBISON. You are my daughter and I have a right to see you.
RHODA. BANG!
ORBISON. Rhoda!

Long pause. RHODA looks around, dips her fingers in the water.

RHODA. Playing much tennis?
ORBISON. No.
RHODA. Me neither.
ORBISON. You were so good.
RHODA. Okay . . .
ORBISON. Better than okay.
RHODA. No, worse if anything.
ORBISON. I miss you terribly.
RHODA. Who is that man in No. 8?
ORBISON *(not looking)*. Bleach.
RHODA. No, I know Bleach. He is one of the few detectives who
thinks a blue shirt passes as disguise.
ORBISON *(casting a glance)*. Don't know.
RHODA. He's watching us.
ORBISON. Is he.

RHODA. He has a look. I think it's the look that comes before a murder. Or indecent exposure. The fixed stare of a defecating dog.
ORBISON. Let's talk.
RHODA. I am talking.
ORBISON. To ME!
RHODA *(leaning back on the cushion, looks coolly up into the sky)*. This isn't working, is it?
ORBISON. Well, of course not. You're not giving it a chance.
RHODA. No. It's abortive. Best thing we can do is lie here till the hour's up, then go our separate ways again.
ORBISON. Rhoda, please . . .
RHODA. Don't call me Rhoda. I hate Rhoda. It's a name they give to queers.
ORBISON. Why do you have to be so relentlessly unkind?
RHODA. It comes over me. The moment I clapped eyes on you, pacing up and down the landing stage, I knew I was going to be rotten to you. Absolutely rotten and dispiriting. *(Pause.)* I should have gone away, of course. But even after two years of absence I hadn't lost my urge to needle you.

Pause.

ORBISON. Come down for the weekend.
RHODA. That man's still there. Nearer if anything.
ORBISON. Bring a boyfriend.
RHODA. I would have thought Bleach shot anyone who came within a dozen yards of you . . .
ORBISON. One weekend. To clear the air.
RHODA *(looks back at* ORBISON*)*. It wouldn't.

Pause.

ORBISON. I do respect you.
RHODA. Oh, don't start that.
ORBISON. I do. I respect your view of me. But I would like the opportunity of changing it.
RHODA. I think you are a poisonous and contaminating woman.
ORBISON. Very well.
RHODA. For all your earnestness. For all your legs-apart, thigh-flashing sincerity. A traitor, and a vile deceiver of good people.
ORBISON. All right.
RHODA. With your sickly air of moderation and good will. It sticks in my throat. It rots my gullet.
ORBISON. Yes.
RHODA. So now you know.
ORBISON. Now I know.
RHODA. He is getting nearer.
ORBISON. Say you'll come.
RHODA. I would be hell.

ORBISON. And I would be heaven.
BLEACH *(off, desperately).* Oi! Look out!

Suddenly a second rowing boat appears right, propelled at full speed by GODBER, *a young man in shirt sleeves. It rams the first boat side on. There is confusion as the occupants try to stay afloat.*

GODBER. Hear me!
RHODA. MUR–DER!
GODBER. Hear me!
ORBISON. I can't swim!
RHODA. MUR–DER!
ORBISON. Shut up! Don't move!
RHODA. MUR–DER! *(She collapses back onto the cushions in a fit of laughter.)*
GODBER. Let me speak! Will you listen!
ORBISON. Could have turned us over! Could have had us in the bloody water!
RHODA *(hands to mouth, laughing).* ASS–ASS–INATION!
ORBISON. Where's Bleach?
RHODA *(looking round).* He's lost an oar.
GODBER. Mrs. Orbison, I have been trailing you all day. I demand you recognise my initiative!
ORBISON. I recognise you are an impertinent little yob, that's all I recognise.
GODBER. Five minutes! Five minutes of your time!
ORBISON. Bleach! Where's Bleach!
RHODA. Going round in circles.
GODBER. I am not armed.
ORBISON *(trying to separate the boats).* Shove off!
GODBER. My name is Michael Godber–
ORBISON. Keep away. Do not come near me! Shove off!

There is a pause while ORBISON *persists in trying to separate the two boats. Neither* RHODA *nor* GODBER *move.*

GODBER. What I have to say won't–
ORBISON. Not listening.
GODBER. I want to offer you–

ORBISON *begins humming loudly and tunelessly to drown his speech.*

RHODA. Ah . . . Bleach has commandeered an oar . . .

They look right as BLEACH *glides on stage in row boat No. 37. He is standing, ill-balanced, in the bows. As his boat gently bumps the stern of* GODBER's, *he takes out a revolver.*

BLEACH. Made it.

ORBISON. You utter fool.
BLEACH. Beg pardon.
ORBISON. Get rid of him.
RHODA. He hasn't told us what he wanted yet.
ORBISON. Bleach.
BLEACH *(to* GODBER*).* Row behind me. Don't try to overtake.
  (He reaches for the oars.)
RHODA. We don't know what he wanted yet!
BLEACH. Fend off.
RHODA. Don't fend off, say something! (GODBER *looks*
  uncertainly from BLEACH *to* RHODA.) Sit down, Bleach.
  (BLEACH *looks at* ORBISON, *then reluctantly sits.)*
GODBER. Thank you. *(He clears his throat.)* I want to be a
  government spy.

Long pause. BLEACH *looks at him.*

ORBISON. I'm afraid there's no such thing.
GODBER *(grinning).* No, well, no, of course there isn't.
ORBISON. No. Really. No such thing.
GODBER. No, but you know—
ORBISON. Not at all.

GODBER *is non-plussed.*

RHODA. That is such balls. *(She looks at* ORBISON.) It is the one
  growth industry. Half the country's sniffing round the arses of the
  other half.
ORBISON. Rhoda.
RHODA. He wants to scramble on the bandwagon, don't you?
  You're out of work and someone told you you could earn a few
  bob sniffing for the government? Licking out the turd of treason?

Pause.

GODBER. If I could give my reasons. By myself.
RHODA *(with a shrug).* Go ahead.
GODBER. Thank you. *(He looks at* ORBISON.) My reasons are
  as follows. *(He takes out a folded sheet of paper and prepares to
  read from it.* RHODA *adjusts her cushions.)*
RHODA. Oh, dear.
GODBER. On my first day at grammar school I was informed that
  I was among the top two and half per cent of England's brains.
  I calculated that this meant only two million people had what I
  had, and a lot of those were senile or the victims of disease. I was
  therefore a leader of society. It seemed obvious I would be
  rewarded appropriately. For example, I could own property.
  I could have a small estate. However, when it came to leaving I
  discovered I had been misled. Although I had the A levels I was
  not invited to become a leader of society. I did not even have

a job. I discovered that the nation was in serious decline. It looked as though nobody would be able to own a small estate. Small estates were looking like things of the past. It was obvious a new society was on the way. *(Pause. He looks up, clears his throat.)* But then it dawned on me, was I ready for the new society? Because when I looked around me, although most people could never have a small estate, there were people who still managed it. In spite of everything, they still had what I dreamed of. And this got me going again. I realised it was part of me. Part of my soul. No matter how small the chance, no one is going to take it away from me. I have my rights. I will not be nobbled by the communists. *(Pause.)* And that is why I would like to be a spy. *(Pause. He folds up the paper, puts it away.)*
RHODA.   My God . . .

A loud-hailer booms.

LOUD HAILER.   Come in, No. 17 . . .
RHODA *(shaking her head at* GODBER*)*.   My God . . .
ORBISON.   All right. I'll put you in touch with someone.
GODBER.   Promise me, Mrs Orbison.
ORBISON.   I will put you in touch with someone. I have said so.
RHODA *(to* GODBER*)*.   You know what you are? You are a grasping, tasteless little shit.
GODBER.   I'm sorry if I happen to have beliefs.
RHODA.   That is not a belief, it's an obscenity.
ORBISON.   Give your name and address to Mr Bleach. And now shove off.
GODBER.   Thank you. I feel sure we'll meet again some time.
(He fends off, rows off enthusiastically, followed by BLEACH.*)*
BLEACH.   Hang about, I'm not in the sodding Sea-scouts . . .
RHODA.   I said we were in for a spot of indecent exposure. I didn't think he'd flash his mind.
GODBER.   You are shocked by the normal aspirations of normal people. It comes of being brought up in an atmosphere of liberal privilege.
RHODA.   Oh, don't come on patrician, Joan.
ORBISON.   They will always disappoint you. With a terrible consistency.
RHODA.   That's what happened to you, is it?
ORBISON.   I could have been a missionary. It ran in our family. But I joined the Labour party instead. And just as missionaries used to suffer as they saw their flock indulge in secret pagan practices so I have suffered, off and on, from glimpses of their inalienable barbarity . . .

They look at one another for some seconds.

RHODA.   I had planned never to see you again. Out of disgust. You know that.

ORBISON. I still have your letter.

RHODA. I thought if people like you could get elected, not once, but time and time again, then democracy had to be a sham, a cheat, an instrument of sloth and poisonous reaction.

ORBISON. All that's in your letter. The precise words.

RHODA. Yes. And I still think so.

ORBISON. Of course.

RHODA. Only more so. Because that creature who was here just now is precisely the kind of monster you create. And that still shocks me.

ORBISON. I am sorry, but at the risk of alienating you still further, I will affirm my belief in our kind of democracy.

RHODA. It is not a democracy. It is a slavish cacophony.

ORBISON. That wasn't in your letter.

RHODA. No. I just thought of it. *(She smiles thinly.)* Not that I love them, or anything. The PEOPLE, I mean. I don't come at the whiff of a donkey jacket. I just cannot stand their apeing the likes of you. And treading on each other's faces.

LOUD HAILER. Come in, No. 17.

ORBISON. They seem to want us.

RHODA. Let them wait.

ORBISON. You will come back? For a weekend?

RHODA. Cop a load of hospitality . . .

LOUD HAILER. No. 17, your time is up.

RHODA. Go on. Before they send a bloody man.

ORBISON *leans to pick up the oars.*
Lights snap out.

Scene Four

A disco pub in London. A few tables and a riot of garish lighting.
Sitting alone at a table, surrounded by bottles and partly drunk,
MCPHEE. *A few tables away,* GODBER, *alone. On a raised dais,*
moving to a slow, lethargic tune, a dancer, SIMONE, *gradually*
removing her bra. MCPHEE, *in deliberate opposition to this, chants*
the chorus of 'Land of a Thousand Dances.'

MCPHEE. La, la-la-la-la, la-la-la-la, la-la-la, la-la-la, OW! Dance to the music! Don't wanna lose it! Got it in my thighbone! Got it in my backbone! I gotta little place! Away across the tracks! Come to my place! I like it like that! Good for yer, Lucy! Keep yer foot loosey! Come to me, Suzy! La, la-la-la-la, la-la-la-la, la-la-la! *(He stops, takes a swig of beer, looks deliberately at* GODBER, *who has been watching* MCPHEE *from the corner of his eye, but now looks resolutely away.* MCPHEE *turns back to* SIMONE.*)* Fuckin' useless! Fuckin' white trash! More like a fuckin' snake charmer, this fuckin' music, this fuckin' whinin' wailin', why doon't yoo move! *(The girl, ignoring MCPHEE, removes her bra with a flourish.)* Oh, fuckin' Jesus, what is that! *(He pretends to cover his eyes.)* OOH! Yoo drivin' me fuckin' mad, yoo are, my temperature's risin', ma jook box is blowin' a fuse! Like fuckin' hell it is! (GODBER *stares ahead.* MCPHEE *persists in looking at him, and as an act of defiance, rises to his feet clutching a bottle in his hand. He begins shaking his hips violently, jerking towards* GODBER's *table in a parody of sexy dancing.)* You gotta know how to pony! Like a bony maron—ey. Mashed potat—o! Oh, do the alligat—or! *(Dragging up his shirt with his free hand to reveal his naked abdomen,* MCPHEE *insinuates himself half across* GODBER's *table.)* Hand over hips! Letcha backbone slip! Do the Wat—usi! Oh, I like yer Lucy! Ow! La, la-la-la-la, la-la-la-la, la-la-la, la-la-la, la, la, la—aa—aaa . . . (GODBER *stoically ignores* MCPHEE, *who suddenly lurches back to his table and sits. The girl is in a contorted position on the dais.)* Yoo fuckin' useless disaster, yoo! Yoo fuckin' apology yoo are! More flesh on Mick Jagger's cakehole! I've seen a fuckin' greyhound wi' diahhorea move better, I have . . . *(He turns to* GODBER, *who is looking deliberately away.)* Oi! *(Pause.)* Oi! Yoo! (GODBER *ignores him.)* Oi! Yoo! Can yoo hear me? Are yoo deaf? *(Reluctantly,* GODBER *turns to him.)* Oh, yoo're not deaf. I thought yoo were deaf. Yoo were just pretendin'. (GODBER *looks away again.)* I said she's a fuckin' bonebag. Did yoo hear what I said? I said . . . *(Pause.)* Would yoo touch that? Would yoo? I would not have that. Yoo can keep that. I would no let that fuckin' near me. I would no, no fuckin' likely! *(Pause, then he yells to the girl.)* Yoo ha' no movement in yer body! Yoo gotta have soul! Soul! Yoo got no soul! *(He leaps up, and jerking out his shirt again, gyrates his hips. He flops back down again, drinks a little, then looks towards* GODBER *again.)* Oi, yoo! Yoo wi' the eyes that do not turn in my direction . . . yoo . . . (GODBER *looks at him.)* Yes, yoo. *(He offers a packet of cigarettes.)* Cigarette? (GODBER *shakes his head.)* Fuck yoo, yoo friendly bastard. *(He lights one himself, then shouts at full volume.)* Mashed pot—ato! Do the allig—ator! *(He turns straight back to* GODBER.) Where am I from? I said where am I from? (GODBER *just looks at him.)* Me! The man on your right who isn't there. Where am I from? *(Pause.)* From fuckin' Jamaica, am I? Do I look Jamaican! Or a fuckin' Hindoo man? I might have soul but I am not from Jamaica! *(Pause, then* GODBER *turns away again.)* Hey. Hey. *(He jerks his head to beckon* GODBER *over, intimately.)* I'm from Scotland. *(Pause.)* Yoo knew! *(Pause.)* Hey. Hey. Are yoo meetin' anybody? Have yoo gotta bird? You gotta bird, have yoo? *(Pause.)* Yoo don't fuckin' say much mate! Talkin' to a fuckin' dummy. Talkin' to a fuckin' mute! *(The music ends.* SIMONE *completes her act in a contorted surrender position on the floor.)* Get off! Get off for Jesus

Christ' sake! *(He covers his eyes mockingly.)* Could turn a geezer
queer, the sight of yer! I think I'm comin' over queer!

SIMONE *gets off the floor, picks up her discarded bra, goes slowly
towards* MCPHEE's *table and stands in front of him. Pause. He opens
his eyes.*

SIMONE.　You dirt. You nothing dirt. *(He looks down, rests on his
knees, hands loosely clasped. Pause.)* Did you hear me? *(Pause. She
screams at him.)* Did you hear me!

Pause. MCPHEE *doesn't move. After some seconds, she turns and
walks out.* MCPHEE *turns directly to* GODBER.

MCPHEE.　I am dossin'. I am at the Wayfaring Hostel of the Holy
Saints. Yoo know it, do yoo? *(Pause.)* Do yoo know the Hostel
of the Holy fuckin' Saints?
GODBER.　Nope.
MCPHEE.　Yoo are nae a dosser, then?
GODBER.　No. I'm not dossing.
MCPHEE.　You got a room? I'm lookin' for a room. You got a room?
GODBER.　Sorry.
MCPHEE.　They are a gang of queers where I'm dossin'. All they are
after is rimmin' yoo. And I am nae a fuckin' rimmer. I want a room.
(Pause.) Have yoo a room?
GODBER.　I just said. No.
MCPHEE.　I'm nae choosey. *(Pause. He suddenly jerks his shoulders.)*
Do the Wat—usi! *(Pause. He sits staring at* GODBER *for some
seconds.)* Paisley to London. In ten hours. *(He jerks his thumb as
if hitching a lift.)* Ten hours. In what I stood up in. To the swingin'
city. To the home of the blues. Doin' the clubs in the evenin' and
dossin' in the day. Great. Fuckin' great. Pink elephant. Whisky a
go-go. Bag o'Nails. Until they fixed me wi' this hostel of the Holy
fuckin' Saints. Are too listenin'? *(*GODBER *nods.)* Well, I'm nae
goin' back there! I am not! Always after rimmin' yoo . . . I want
a room!

Enter KNATCHBULL, *in an open overcoat, clutching a bag and a glass
of whisky.*

KNATCHBULL.　Hello, Billy. Watching the girls?
MCPHEE.　No fuckin' dancer, she is not.
KNATCHBULL.　No rhythm, eh? No soul? Get us a chair. *(He looks
at* GODBER *as* MCPHEE *crosses to the next table and fetches a
chair.)* Would you be Mr. Godber?
GODBER.　That's right.

Pause. KNATCHBULL *smiles, extends a hand.*

KNATCHBULL.　Knatchbull. *(Lighting changes from garish coloured
lamps to a dull daytime quality. It is past closing time, late in the*

afternoon. GODBER, MCPHEE *and* KNATCHBULL *are at the same table.)* There was a time we were all public schoolboys in this game. You're not a public schoolboy, Mr. Godber? No? I'm glad. We were recruited from the bar stalls of Whites and Boodles and we were very fucking obvious. We were a little bit queer too, which didn't help. It wasn't very satisfactory on the whole. Since then the grammar school element has crept in, with tangible benefits to all concerned. Have you had education, Mr Godber?

GODBER. I fit the bill exactly.

KNATCHBULL. Not too much and not too little? (GODBER *nods.)* That's lovely. That's spot on.

MCPHEE. About my room . . .

KNATCHBULL. Hold on, Billy.

MCPHEE. I need a room.

KNATCHBULL. Put a sock in it, there's a lad.

GODBER. Is he with you?

KNATCHBULL. We have occasion to employ him, yes. We don't draw all our water from one well. We have travelled light years since the old school tie was the criterion of reliability. *(He smiles.)* Are you a patriotic man, Mr Godber? *(Pause.)* By which I mean. . . *(Pause.)* Well, I think you know what I mean.

GODBER. I think so, yes.

KNATCHBULL. You think so.

GODBER. I think I know what you mean.

KNATCHBULL. Yes. Well.

Pause.

GODBER. I am.

KNATCHBULL. Glad to hear it. I only ask because. . . *(Pause. He grins.)* You'd be bloody silly if you said no, wouldn't you? You would be a silly berk. *(Pause.)* Funny, though, some of us, the public schoolboys, weren't always patriotic. Sitting on the bar stalls, we would shoot our mouths off. In the Athanaeum. How we preferred the Russians. Biting the hand that fed us. Pissing on the altar and what not. Why do you want to be an agent, Mr Godber?

MCPHEE. Because he's fuckin' skint, that's why!

KNATCHBULL. Thank you, Billy.

MCPHEE. Ask a silly question.

KNATCHBULL. Any reasons, Mr Godber? Or may I call you Michael?

MCPHEE. Call him Michael, for fuck's sake.

Pause.

KNATCHBULL. Well, Michael?

Pause.

GODBER.   In a few words—
KNATCHBULL.   If you would, please.

Pause.

GODBER.   It thrills me.

Pause.

KNATCHBULL.   Well, well. *(Pause.)* Well, well. *(Pause.)* I like that.
   Yes, that's perfect. It's what got Hilary on Everest, after all.
   It's what got Scott down the Antartic. I'm not disinclined to
   you for that.
GODBER.   Thank you.
KNATCHBULL.   But we do have our disasters, Michael. I would
   not be being honest with you if I pretended we do not have
   disasters. It's not all peaches and cream.
GODBER.   I don't think I'd enjoy it, Mr Knatchbull, if it were.
KNATCHBULL.   No spice, eh?
GODBER.   That's right.
KNATCHBULL.   I like that. I like that angle, Michael. Not every-
   one we have to do with has that spirit of adventure. It is on
   the decrease, I would say. It's all types now, isn't it, Billy?
   What you can get?
MCPHEE.   Lucky dip.
KNATCHBULL.   Not that it was any different when we were
   public schoolboys, I suppose. We were liquorice allsorts just
   the same. Only we were a tiny bit queer with it, which didn't
   help. *(Pause.)* Not that way inclined yourself, are you? I only
   ask because—*(Pause.)* I only ask.
GODBER.   I have yet to discover it.
KNATCHBULL.   Good answer. Always worried about people who
   are too affirmative. There is no definite line to be drawn where
   the sexual inclinations are concerned, so psychiatrists tell us.
   Isn't that so?
MCPHEE.   It is so.
KNATCHBULL.   Billy knows.
MCPHEE.   I fuckin' do.
KNATCHBULL.   So there we are, then. I think that's all. *(Pause.
   He smiles at* GODBER.)
GODBER.   That's all?
KNATCHBULL.   As far as I'm concerned.
GODBER.   Don't I have to be thoroughly screened?
MCPHEE.   What's that?
KNATCHBULL.   Oh, you have done your homework. I like a
   man who comes prepared.
MCPHEE.   Thinks he's in the CIA.
KNATCHBULL.   I like that. It shows initiative.
GODBER.   I could be a double agent. I could be a traitor.

KNATCHBULL.   Oh yes, you could. That is a valid point. And take
   it from me, this screening as you call it does go on. But in the
   meantime I would like you out there. On a job. We want our
   people in the field. Like honeybees. Gathering, delivering and
   gathering again.
MCPHEE.   More bees than fuckin' flowers as far as I can see.
KNATCHBULL.   I wouldn't say that Billy, from my vantage point.
MCPHEE.   All bees down the Claimants Union. I ha' had a bellyful
   o' the Claimants Union.
KNATCHBULL.   I'm sure you have, and I was coming to that.
MCPHEE.   I wanna move.
KNATCHBULL.   I was coming to that. If you would listen.
MCPHEE.   I am listenin'. But I am also tellin' yoo that I ha' had
   a bellyful of hostels and Claimants fuckin' Unions. I wanna room.
   I ha' been treated like dogshit and I wanna room!
KNATCHBULL.   Not all peaches and cream you see, Michael.
MCPHEE.   Have I been good or have I not?
KNATCHBULL.   You have been, and I have made a note of it.
   Nothing done for me goes unappreciated.
MCPHEE.   Yoo could ha' fooled me.
KNATCHBULL.   Billy, let a bloke get a word in.
MCPHEE.   I'm nae stoppin' yoo, I am just layin' it down what I
   want, what I am after. I've had enough.
KNATCHBULL.   Thank you. *(Pause.)* As I was saying, we like
   our people out and about. Any dirt comes out in the wash, rest
   assured on that one. *(He opens his bag.)* Now Michael, do you
   know this man? *(He holds up a photograph. Pause.)*
GODBER.   No.
KNATCHBULL.   All right. There is a pub in Lambeth called the
   Oakleigh Arms. It is a one-eyed pub, not the sort of establishment
   you would expect to be patronized by an officer from
   Knightsbridge barracks, unless in search of bumboys, which he
   may be for all I know. Start drinking there will you, Michael?
   And Billy here, who is so sick of Claimants Unions, he'll be in
   there on and off. And bring your honeybags to me. I'm the
   queen bee, Michael. I lie there, on my fat arse, while you feed me.
   Understand? *(He stands up, closing his case.)*
MCPHEE.   About me, Mr Knatchbull—
KNATCHBULL.   I have you in mind, Billy.
MCPHEE.   Maybe you have, but—
KNATCHBULL.   I have you very much in mind. *(He turns to*
   GODBER.) Goodbye, Michael. Don't get up. *(He shakes his*
   hand.) Did I tell you my daughter was a spina bifida?
GODBER.   No. I am sorry.
KNATCHBULL.   But very bright. *(He taps his temple.)* All there.
   (GODBER *nods.)* It's her birthday.
GODBER.   Oh?

KNATCHBULL. She's eight. (GODBER *nods.)* Got kids?
GODBER. No.
KNATCHBULL. I recommend 'em. A blessing.
GODBER. Yes. So they say.

The spot isolates KNATCHBULL *again.*

KNATCHBULL. He sits there, tingling like a splash of aftershave.
  And all the time the treason's steaming off him, like hot piss out
  of some old incontinent. . .

The spot disappears. KNATCHBULL *goes out. Long pause.*

MCPHEE. Are yoo gonna be my mate? *(He tips his chair onto its
  back legs. Pause.)*
GODBER. I don't see why not.
MCPHEE. Yoo don't see why not. Ta for your enthusiasm.
GODBER. I'll be your mate.

Pause. MCPHEE *looks at him for some seconds.*

MCPHEE. All right. That's good. I have no mates. Yoo are my
  first mate.
GODBER. I'm honoured.
MCPHEE. Yoo are. I don't spread maself around. When I say yoo
  are my mate, it's no half fuckin' serious. It's life or death wi' me,
  I'm tellin' yoo. It's blood brotherhood.
GODBER. No half-measures.
MCPHEE. No fuckin' likely. It's for keeps. *(Pause.)* So I ask yoo
  again. Do yoo wanna be my mate?

Pause.

GODBER. Yes.
MCPHEE *(rolling up his sleeve).* Roll up yer sleeve.
GODBER. What for?
MCPHEE. Roll up yer sleeve.
GODBER. We'll shake on it.
MCPHEE. Yoo shake hands wi' him, yoo shake hands wi' anybody.
  I'm nae takin' a mate on a handshake.·
GODBER *(rolling up his sleeve reluctantly).* This is necessary, is it?
MCPHEE. Jesus! Do yoo wanna be my mate or not! *(Pause.*
  GODBER *nods.* MCPHEE *takes out a long-bladed knife and
  gashes his own arm. Pause.)* Shall I nick yoo, or do yoo wanna nick
  yersel'? (GODBER *shrugs. He lays his bared arm on the table.*
  MCPHEE *nicks him with the blade, then lays his own wound on
  GODBER's. Pause.)* Yoo stick by me. I stick by yoo.
GODBER. Okay.

MCPHEE *rolls down his sleeve, looking at* GODBER *all the time.*

MCPHEE *(grinning).* Now, wha's the situation wi' this room?

Blackout.

Scene Five

The back lawn of ORBISON's *home in Berkshire.* ORBISON
and RHODA *are playing Jokari in the sun. They speak between shots.*

RHODA. Got a man?

ORBISON. I've got Trevor.

RHODA. And you fuck.

ORBISON. Reads T.S. Eliot.

RHODA. Before or after?

ORBISON. Unimportant.

RHODA. Vital.

ORBISON. It is not. *(She misses the return. The ball bounces about.)*
Really, it isn't. *(She looks at* RHODA, *throws down the bat,
goes to pour an orange juice.)*

RHODA. I was living in Tooting. Did you look for me there?

ORBISON. There's a common, isn't there?

RHODA. Yes. Horse-rides and gang bangs, and a nice light soil for
scraping shallow graves. *(She sits in a deck-chair.)* I had a
thoroughly squalid bedsitter, directly opposite the mental
hospital. Only at first I thought it was a factory. So the first night
I was there I didn't pull the curtains. You know how I hate
curtains. I undressed with the window bare. It was only when I
switched off the light I noticed it. The corridor across the road,
jam-packed with patients and male nurses, pressed against the
bars, all gazing down at me. And because they couldn't see any
more, they drifted away in ones and twos like people leaving a
cinema. The next morning I discovered there had been a woman in
this room before me. *(Pause.)* So I was faced with this decision,
whether to keep up the precedent, or finish it, and draw the
curtains when I went to bed. (ORBISON *looks at her.)* I kept it
up. Of course I was self-conscious to begin with. Then it came quite
naturally.

ORBISON. You're lucky you weren't murdered. One of them might
have broken out and murdered you.

RHODA. I thought it was worth it. In view of the obvious benefit
to all those people. *(Pause.)* In any case, there was a whacking
great bolt on the door. My predecessor must have thought of that.

ORBISON. And what about them? Did you wonder what you
might have done to them?

RHODA. Well, that rather depends on who took over from me,
doesn't it?

ORBISON. You tortured them.

RHODA. Stop flattering me.

ORBISON. You tortured them.

RHODA. Don't come on with your piety! Don't dare! *(Pause.)*
You with your government. And that vile building I thought was a

factory. Don't dare. *(She stares at* ORBISON. *Pause.)* Christ, it's
hot. . .

Pause.

ORBISON.   I'm expecting someone in a minute.
RHODA.   Shall I piss off?
ORBISON.   No, of course not. This is your home.
RHODA.   Home is where the hurt is. . .
ORBISON.   That's up to you. *(She turns to go.)*
RHODA.   It's difficult, but I don't think we should separate the
good man from his evil works, do you? *(Pause.)* To take you,
for example. You have such an abundancy of private goodness,
don't you?
ORBISON.   Do I?
RHODA.   Yes. But the creature who ran Auschwitz was a perfect
family man. I don't think we should ever forget that, do you?
ORBISON.   No, never. *(She looks at* RHODA.) You have to be
careful with disgust. It is so deceptive, if often tricks you into
thinking it is radical. When all the time it is some strangled cry
for feeling at any price. Which is not the same thing is it?

Pause. RHODA *smiles sarcastically.* ORBISON *goes out.* RHODA
yawns and stretches. KNATCHBULL *enters unobserved, stops. He
sees* RHODA *but does not announce himself.* RHODA *gets up and
idly wanders to pour an orange juice. As she turns to come back, she
sees him.*

KNATCHBULL.   Oh. (RHODA *takes him in, sits in the deck-chair.)*
She was in the garden, I was told. (RHODA *just sips.)* Is she?
(Pause. KNATCHBULL *tears his eyes away, sees the Jokari set.
He picks up the bat, makes a vague swipe.)* I have a daughter.
(Pause.) Spina bifida. *(He looks at* RHODA, *who does not react.)*
Unfortunately. *(He strikes the ball.)* Is this your set, then?
RHODA.   Why don't you go and look for her?
KNATCHBULL.   Yes. *(He doesn't move, just looks at her.)*
RHODA.   Haven't you seen a girl before? *(He stares at her.)*
Piss off, will you.
KNATCHBULL *(weightily).*   I come here every Thursday. Dead on
three.
RHODA.   Ah. Bear that in mind.
KNATCHBULL.   Knatchbull.
RHODA.   Okay. Knatchbull.

ORBISON *comes in.*

ORBISON.   You found your own way.
KNATCHBULL *(gazing around).*   Very pleasant, your part of the
country. . .
RHODA.   It's not hers. (KNATCHBULL *looks at* ORBISON.) She's

not a baron. It's not her fief. *(They look at her. She gets up.)*
The way he said it. . . *(She picks up a cardigan, goes out.)*
KNATCHBULL *(puts down the Jokari bat and opens his bag. He takes out a photograph).* I wonder if you know this man?
ORBISON. No.
KNATCHBULL *(taking another).* Or him?
ORBISON. No.
KNATCHBULL. What about this one?
ORBISON. It's a back view.
KNATCHBULL *(examining it).* Oh yes. Taken from a car.
ORBISON. Well, really, I don't see how I can be expected—
KNATCHBULL. Silly buggers aren't they, photographers? Ask for a close-up and they give you a picture of his arse. *(He stuffs them back in the bag.)*
ORBISON. Anyway, these snapshots never mean a thing to me.
KNATCHBULL. No. . . Only sometimes these characters turn out to be on the weekend party circuit.
ORBISON. Not on mine.
KNATCHBULL. Gin and tonic wallahs.
ORBISON. I do think we have got to keep this in proportion. I really do.
KNATCHBULL. Absolutely.
ORBISON. I do think, whilst I recognize we are facing an unprecedented crisis—
KNATCHBULL. Hear, hear!
ORBISON. Can I finish?
KNATCHBULL. Sorry.
ORBISON. That there is a danger we are making an obsession out of conspiracy. We don't want to end up like Brazil, do we? *(Pause.)* Do we?
KNATCHBULL. Brazil?
ORBISON. For Christ's sake, Knatchbull.
KNATCHBULL. We are only acting in response.
ORBISON. That expression has about as much definition as piss on blotting paper.
KNATCHBULL. I'm sorry about my expressions. I'll try and do better.
ORBISON. We must not manufacture it. Do you understand me? We must not breed a race of agents provocateurs.
KNATCHBULL. Oh, those. The story-book monstrosities.
ORBISON. Yes, those.
KNATCHBULL. I don't think there is any danger.
ORBISON. Our system relies entirely on consent. On confidence. I do not want that confidence eroded, because there comes a time when the game is no longer worth the candle. Quite simply. When the scaffolding obliterates the edifice.
KNATCHBULL. I see that, yes.

ORBISON. I am terrified of mayhem. No matter who it comes from. I will not have it. Do you understand?

KNATCHBULL. I receive you loud and clear.

ORBISON. I'm glad.

KNATCHBULL. All right. *(Pause.)* But you see, there is a lot of conspiracy going on. I dunno why. Search me what they are getting so het up about. But it is going on. No doubt about it. And these pictures prove it.

ORBISON. Prove it?

KNATCHBULL. Proof, suspicion, call it what you like—the point is, we have got to have the information or there will be mayhem, as you call it. Real mayhem, which you are quite rightly bothered about. *(Pause.)* And that's what I am after stopping, and that's what you have got to tell 'em, when they niggle you at Question Time.

ORBISON. I do. Consistently.

KNATCHBULL. The Brazilians, to whom you made reference just now, they have their own Brazilian way of doing things. It's not in our character, is it? This Death Squad business. It's very foreign. It's Latin, isn't it? Or Indian, is it? I dunno. But anyway their racial mixture has produced a highly violent level of response.

ORBISON. I don't care for this term response.

KNATCHBULL. You do know what I mean, though.

ORBISON. Do make a point of examining your language.

KNATCHBULL. All right.

ORBISON. Don't do violence to language or you will end up doing violence to people.

KNATCHBULL. To get back to these photographs. . .

ORBISON. That is not an academic point.

Pause. He looks at her. Then he takes out another photograph.

KNATCHBULL. This gentleman is in the Coldstream Guards.

ORBISON. Yes.

KNATCHBULL *(handing it to her).* An officer.

ORBISON. An officer.

KNATCHBULL. A Major.

ORBISON. A Major.

Pause. He scrutinizes her.

KNATCHBULL. I am sorry if this gets up your nose, Home Secretary, but I have very clear instructions to keep you briefed. To stop the mayhem and so on.

ORBISON. I'm sorry.

KNATCHBULL. It's a very tiring journey from Whitehall.

ORBISON. Yes. I am sorry.

Pause.

KNATCHBULL.   Okay. This Major has served in Ireland. Possibly
a bit too long.
ORBISON.   Meaning?
KNATCHBULL.   He has friendships in the ranks.

Pause. She smiles.

ORBISON.   Yes, but . . .
KNATCHBULL.   It isn't funny, Mrs. Orbison. It isn't really. Not
at all.

She still smiles.

ORBISON.   I do not see what—
KNATCHBULL.   Mrs Orbison, I know you are a Labour minister
and we all pooh-pooh class nowadays—
ORBISON.   You don't have to use that tone with me.
KNATCHBULL.   All right—
ORBISON.   I am deadly serious.

Pause. He stands with his hands on his hips, looking down.

KNATCHBULL.   Oh, dear. Dear me. *(Pause.)* He drinks with rankers,
Mrs Orbison.
ORBISON.   Yes.

Pause.

KNATCHBULL.   Which means . . . ? *(He looks at her. She is blank.)*
Which means? Two things. Right?
ORBISON.   You are leaps ahead of me.
KNATCHBULL.   He's queer. Or he has gone political.
ORBISON.   Ah. That's the way, is it? *(He nods.)* Ah.
KNATCHBULL.   Very important thing, the army. Could be all that
stood between us and—whatever. In the last resort, that is. *(He
looks intently at her.)*
ORBISON.   Let me assure you, if it was—the only thing that stood
between *us,* as you put it, and whatever—I might end up supporting
the whatever. I don't go overboard for military dictatorships.
KNATCHBULL.   Me neither, naturally, but I do think . . . the army
is the army, Mrs. Orbison!

Pause.

ORBISON.   I agree. Wholeheartedly.
KNATCHBULL.   Phew. *(He grins.)* So I am watching Major Cadbury.
ORBISON.   Yes.
KNATCHBULL.   And I am using Mr. Godber.
ORBISON.   Is that a name I should be familiar with?
KNATCHBULL.   He's a dab hand at rowing, is our Michael. I
understand you met him on the Serpentine.
ORBISON.   You're using *him?*

KNATCHBULL. I chuck 'em all in, good and bad. And out of the steaming compost comes the fat fruit of a conspiracy.
ORBISON. The poetry of putrefaction. . .

KNATCHBULL *shuts his bag with a click.*

KNATCHBULL. I think you're squeamish, Mrs Orbison.
ORBISON. Not so squeamish I prefer to be kept in the dark.
KNATCHBULL *(smiling, turning to go, looking over the country).* It is so very pleasant here. It really is. *(He walks a little way, stops.)* You know, when these people go on about privilege, I suppose they must mean you. . . *(He grins.)*

Blackout.

Scene Six

A dismal room, lit from the street. A single bed, containing
GODBER. *On the floor on a mattress,* MCPHEE, *smoking.*

MCPHEE. This is heaven, this is. *(Pause.)* I believe in God, but I don't care what he's got on offer, this is heaven, this is. *(Pause.)* Are yoo asleep?
GODBER. Nope.
MCPHEE. I love this. Yoo and me here. It can be pissin' doon outside, there can be fuckin' murder goin' on, but we're fine. *(Pause.)* You are naturally quiet, aren't yoo? Ye're noo windbag.
GODBER. I listen, but I don't talk. And when I meet people, I think, you are a bastard, now prove to me otherwise.
MCPHEE. An' do they make the effort?
GODBER. It has been known.
MCPHEE. I'm nae bothered. I admire yoo. I admire people who keep themselves to themselves. I respect that. Everybody's bein' so fuckin' intimate nowadays. *(Pause.)* Mind yoo, I like a laugh. *(Pause.)* And sex. I goo for that in a big way. There's noo stoppin' me when the mood is on. I am a fuckin' blitzkrieg when the mood is on. *(Pause.)* I have had women against their will. *(Pause.)* Did you hear me?
GODBER. I heard you.
MCPHEE. On the ground. A fuckin' wet thing on the ground.

Light goes out on the bed-sit and comes up on a car, dimly lit. Inside vague shapes behind misted windows.

ADJABS. Bill—y!

Two youths appear from behind the car, where they have been kneeling. MCPHEE *appears, stands some yards away.*

JUMBO. Well, wha' are we waitin' for? *(Pause.)* Christ, ha' we not talked about this! *(None of them moves.)* Fuckin' hell!

With a violent movement he grabs the door handle of the car.
ADJABS *follows suit, but* BILLY *just watches as they try to drag the occupants out.*

WOMAN. Let go of me! You dirty little bastard, will you let go of me!
ADJABS *(to* MCPHEE). Don't just stand there!
MAN. We're not moving.
JUMBO. Get oot, you fuckin' dirty cow.
MAN. We have done absolutely nothing to you. We don't know you.
ADJABS. Fuckin' get oot!
MAN. Tell us what we've done and maybe we—
WOMAN *(as* JUMBO *grabs her).* Oh, Christ! *(She screams.)*
MAN. Look, you are being so bloody silly, you really are.
ADJABS *(to* MCPHEE). Help us!
MAN. We are not getting out.
WOMAN. No, please! Look, no!
JUMBO. No fuckin' clothes on. Not a fuckin' stitch on!
MAN. It's no good, you know. We're not moving.
JUMBO. Let go of the fuckin' steerin' wheel. You filth. You fuckin' filth!
MAN. Do tell us when you've finished.

ADJABS *knees him in the face. He groans. Falls forward onto the steering wheel.*

WOMAN. Oh, Christ!
JUMBO *(pulling her out of the car).* Naked! Fuckin' naked wi' a man!
ADJABS. Beautiful! Oh, beautiful!
JUMBO *(contemplating the* WOMAN *on the ground).* Dirty. Naked. Spunked-up filth. *(He begins undoing his trousers.)*
WOMAN. Please. . . look . . . PLEASE!
ADJABS. Begging for it. Can't get enough.
JUMBO. All runnin' wi' his spunk in her. All wet from him. *(He sinks to his knees beside her.)* Oh Christ, darling, I could murder you. . .

As JUMBO *rapes her,* ADJABS, *undoing his belt, looks round to* MCPHEE, *who hasn't moved.*

ADJABS. Billy! *(He doesn't move.)* Well, do you want it or not! *(Pause.)* Are you a mate!

Hesitating a second, MCPHEE *joins them. They all kneel over the woman.*

JUMBO. We did it! We did it!

ADJABS. We did it! We did it!

With an explosion of relief they all burst out giggling, arms around each other's necks.

JUMBO.
ADJABS. } *(in unison).* We did it! We did it! We did it! We did it!
MCPHEE.

They collapse in long, hysterical laughter. Suddenly, powerful torches bathe them in light. They stop at once, blink.

JUMBO. Wha's the—
MCPHEE *(shading his eyes).* Hey . . . *(They look from side to side. A number of POLICEMEN enter, forming a distant semi-circle. KNATCHBULL enters, holding an alsatian on a lead. He stops. He remains standing in a strange light, then raising his free hand, he beckons to MCPHEE with a finger.)* Christ . . .

Slowly, naked from the waist down, MCPHEE rises and crosses the stage. He stops a few feet from KNATCHBULL, then he falls to his knees. KNATCHBULL goes over to the WOMAN, who is lying on the ground, sobbing. He looks at her.

KNATCHBULL. That's right . . . that's right . . . all right . . .
WOMAN. I had a ticket to Australia . . . I could have got out to Australia . . . !
KNATCHBULL. Those were the days. No one wants to take us now.
WOMAN. This bloody country! I HATE THIS PLACE!

Pause.

KNATCHBULL. We do our best . . .
WOMAN. I HATE THIS PLACE!

She breaks down sobbing again. KNATCHBULL watches for a moment, looks around to his men.

KNATCHBULL. Has no one got a blanket here! *(A POLICEMAN covers the WOMAN. KNATCHBULL, collecting a dog's collar and lead from a second POLICEMAN, walks over to where MCPHEE is kneeling and attaches it to his neck.)* You be my dog now, Billy. You bark when I bark, you sniff where I sniff. *(Pause.)* Woof! Woof!
MCPHEE. Aye . . .
KNATCHBULL. Woof! Woof!
MCPHEE. All right . . .
KNATCHBULL. Woof! Woof!
MCPHEE. Woof. Woof.

KNATCHBULL. ⎫
MCPHEE.   ⎬ Woof, woof! Woof, woof!

They bark together for some seconds, MCPHEE *stopping when*
KNATCHBULL *stops. The lights go off and come up on the bed-sit.*

MCPHEE.   An' I ha' nae touched a woman since that day. I ha'
    been dossin' wi' dossers an' rimmin' wi' rimmers, all for Mr
    Knatchbull.
GODBER.   What do you tell him?
MCPHEE.   I start up conversation wi' any dosser who is no a
    regular. An' if they say somethin' like the food is shit, I tell him they
    are communists. An' if they doon't say nothin', I still say they
    are communists, but very fuckin' circumspect.

Pause.

GODBER.   I like spying Billy, I'm afraid. I hope you won't mind
    that. I hope it won't come between us.
MCPHEE.   Why should it?
GODBER.   I can't think.
MCPHEE.   Yoo don't criticize yer mates. Whatever they do, tha's
    their scene. But when they come to yoo, yoo stick by 'em.
    I had ma throat slashed because I would na' tell some lads where
    my last mate was holed up. An' all the time he was fuckin'
    double crossin' me.
GODBER.   You have suffered.
MCPHEE.   I have had bad mates. Life is a series of bad mates.
GODBER.   Yet you persevere . . .
MCPHEE.   I ha' nae learned my lesson. I will no believe that life
    is nothin' but a pan of piss. When I find that oot, then I don't
    care if I'm dead or not.
GODBER.   I see.
MCPHEE.   Yoo don't have to agree wi' me.
GODBER.   I don't.
MCPHEE.   Well, wha' do yoo believe in, then? *(Pause.)* I said wha'
    do yoo believe in?
GODBER.   In cutting ice. *(Pause.)* In all this falling down of
    everything. In this howling wind that all the good old souls are
    struggling in, staggering from wall to wall, lurching to the great
    Calcutta of the future. In all this chewing and spewing and spitting
    out of people. I believe in cutting ice.
MCPHEE.   How?
GODBER.   Down here. In the alleys and the pubs. In the new rage
    of street politics. I am going to be a star, Billy. And you can be
    my roadie if you like.

Pause. MCPHEE's *cigarette glows in the gloom.*

GODBER.   You certainly snap up an offer. Like a seal at feeding
time.

MCPHEE.   I wud like to be your roadie! *(Pause.)* Yoo know I wud.
Only I ha' nae come clean wi' yoo.

GODBER.   Go on.

MCPHEE.   Promise you will nae boot me outta here.

GODBER.   We're mates, aren't we?

MCPHEE.   Gi' me your word.

GODBER.   I will not boot you out of here.

Pause.

MCPHEE.   I fancy yoo. *(Long pause.)* I cud no carry on without
yoo knowin'! I keep no secrets from my mates.

Pause.

GODBER.   I want to put the light on.

MCPHEE.   I'm no gonna jump on yoo.

GODBER.   I want to put the light on. *(He switches on a side-
lamp, sits up.)*

MCPHEE.   Yoo nae reciprocate the feeling, I assume. *(Pause.)*
Well, tha's okay. I'm no hurt. I reckon I can live wi' it.

GODBER.   I have no leanings in that direction, Billy. None
at all.

MCPHEE.   Well, tha's okay.

GODBER.   There are all kinds of things I am not party to.
Wonderful things, no doubt. Ineffable delights like buggery.
But they don't touch me. You could pack my pleasures in a
matchbox. What I want, I do want. The rest is rat's piss as far
as I'm concerned.

MCPHEE.   I believe yoo. Yoo are very steely-eyed, yoo are. I
think yoo are goin' to be somebody. *(Pause.)* An' I also believe
that what yoo want, I have nae even dreamed of. I think the
things yoo want would blow a fuckin' great hole through the
minds of ordinary geezers. *(Pause.)* I admire yoo . . .

GODBER.   So that's cleared up then, is it?

MCPHEE.   I wud say so . . .

GODBER.   Good. Now maybe we can get some kip.

Blackout.

Scene Seven

*A windy day on Wimbledon Common. KNATCHBULL in an open
overcoat is controlling a kite, gazing upwards as he wanders slowly
downstage. Standing watching him, his paraplegic daughter,
VERITY.*

KNATCHBULL. Well, this is fun. *(Pause.)* This is a lovely day out. *(Pause.)* What do you say? *(Pause. He looks back quickly over his shoulder.)* Fun, is it? Does she say it's fun? *(Pause.)* Verity. *(She doesn't reply. KNATCHBULL crosses further downstage, tugging at the kite string.)* Do you want an ice-cream? *(Pause.)* Say when you want one. *(Pause.)* Sweetheart. *(The kite loses height. He jerks the string more violently.)* Hello, hello . . . *(He struggles to keep it aloft.)* Come on . . . *(Pause.)* More wind! *(He starts to run to lift the kite. As he does so, the dead body of the soldier MICK HAYMAN appears directly in his path. He trips over it. The kite comes slowly down. Slowly, KNATCHBULL picks himself up onto his knees, gazing at the corpse. VERITY begins to come over to him.)* Don't come. *(He gets up, steps back.)* Stay there, sweetheart. *(She continues to approach.)* Don't come!
VERITY *(arriving beside him).* Shot through the head.
KNATCHBULL. Don't look.
VERITY. Through the back of the head.
KNATCHBULL. He's sleeping, that's all. You wait over there.
VERITY. Was he tortured?
KNATCHBULL. Pick some flowers. Make daddy a daisy chain.

She doesn't move. He looks at her, as with her head on one side, she reads the name on his jacket.

VERITY. Cold . . . stream . . . Guards . . .
KNATCHBULL. Very good.
VERITY *(looks at him, grins. Then turns back).* Are those burns on his fingers?
KNATCHBULL *(rising to his feet).* These bloody great commons. In the middle of London. Great acres of nothing. Dogs shitting, suicides, couples undressed. *(Pause.)* Where can a father walk with his kid!

Pause.

VERITY. Are those cuts made with razors, do you think? *(Pause.)* Or bowie knives?

He looks at her a moment, then goes to her, takes her head in his hands and pulls her to him.

KNATCHBULL. No childhood. *(Pause.)* No proper bloody childhood any more. *(She stays quite still in his arms. Pause.)* Do you love me?
VERITY. Yes.
KNATCHBULL. Promise me.
VERITY. I do! *(Pause, then he lets her go and removes his overcoat to cover the body.)* Do you remember that dog that got washed up on the beach on holiday? It was all stiff, with no eyes.

KNATCHBULL *(covering the body)*.   You've always liked dead
things, Christ knows why.

VERITY.   Dear mongrel, I kept saying, where have you been?
How did you come to end up in the sea?

KNATCHBULL.   I blame the television. All this viewing. If I was
a better father I'd stop it. Make you read. *(He gets up, dusts
his hands.)*

VERITY.   Like this man. Where did he come from? How did he
die?

KNATCHBULL *holds out a hand to lead her away.*

KNATCHBULL.   Ah well, if we knew that . . .

CORPSE.   HE DOES KNOW THAT!

KNATCHBULL.   All right? Leave the kite here, help the police to
spot it.

CORPSE.   WHERE I CAME FROM. HOW I DIED.

KNATCHBULL.   Come on, sweetheart.

CORPSE.   THEY INFILTRATED US. I WENT TO WARN HIM
AT THE PUB.

VERITY.   Warn who?

CORPSE.   THE MAJOR.

VERITY.   The Major?

CORPSE.   AT THE OAKLEIGH ARMS!

VERITY.   What's that?

CORPSE.   OH CHRIST!

KNATCHBULL.   Come on . . .

VERITY.   I'm sorry, but you—

CORPSE.   THEY TIED ME TO A CHAIR. POURED PETROL
UP MY NOSTRILS. TWISTED COMBS IN MY HAIR.

VERITY.   That rhymes!

CORPSE.   I DID NOT SPEAK! I HAVE NEVER KNOWN SUCH
PAIN. TELL THEM I NEVER SPOKE.

KNATCHBULL.   Verity. Sweetheart.

VERITY.   I'm sorry, I've got to go.

CORPSE.   TELL SOMEBODY ABOUT MY PAIN!

*Pause, then she turns to KNATCHBULL. He has his hands on his hips
and is looking at her quizzically.*

KNATCHBULL.   All right? *(She goes to him. He puts an arm on
her shoulder.)* Let's get an ice-cream.

They walk away. Lights fade to black.

ACT TWO

Scene One

The public bar of the Oakleigh Arms, Lambeth. A woman, spot-lit is alone behind the bar, wiping glasses.

NADINE. I never let 'em take their socks off. I was very strict
on that. If they went to take their socks off I'd say DARLING,
IT IS NOT YOUR FEET I'M MASSAGING. Shoes, yes, because
I have the bedspread to consider, but I have no wish to see your
veiny feet. Apart from the smell there is the element of
Athlete's Foot, and no girl wants that along with all the other
risks. *(Pause.)* So when my Major said he wanted to be
NAKED I pooh-poohed him, tried to jostle him along a bit. And
he said MISS, YOU ARE DEGRADING ME. Degrading you?
Aren't you degrading me, I said, talking of degrading? I am the
one who is degraded, not you. And he said, ever so calmly,
nothing that is human is degrading, except we make it so. And
I must admit I liked that. I thought he was a bit of a philosopher,
and you don't find many of them in the army. *(Pause.)* We came
to an arrangement in the end. He gave me seven quid instead of
five, and we did it in the altogether. And later, when I got to
know him, it would happen in the bed, actually in it, in the
sheets, a thing I had reserved entirely for my husband, like the
kissing of nipples, which he had too, in time. *(Pause.)* When I
gave up massage, planning to retire to Brighton, he fixed me
and the old man with a license for this pub, through a fellow
officer whose family runs a brewery. Just to keep me handy.
For what he calls accessibility.

Enter SOLDIERS *carrying chairs and drinks. Lights up on the
public bar.*

TELLING. The point is this—
HART. We know your point!
TELLING. The point is this!
HART. We know.
EDEN. Sit down, sit down . . .
TELLING. I won't sit down, Roy, thank you.
MURPHY. Let him say it.
TELLING. A man is dead.
HART. We know.
TELLING. A man is dead. A comrade is dead. And it is open house
here. A comrade has been murdered—
MURPHY. We don't know that.
TELLING. He has been murdered!

33

MURPHY. We don't know that.

TELLING. Fucking hell! We don't know, we do know, I tell you we do know. What are you after, a signed confession from the Chief Commissioner? The point is that we do know. They are onto us, and it is open house here!

EDEN. What are you saying.

TELLING. I am saying we have got to put an end to it. Shut a few doors. Close a few windows. We have got to have security.

MURPHY. Wait for Cadbury.

TELLING. Wait for Cadbury, wait for Cadbury! I will talk to Cadbury. When he condescends to turn up, I will talk to him.

NADINE. Don't knock him. Not in my bar.

TELLING. Who's knocking him?

NADINE. You are.

TELLING. Not knocking him.

NADINE. Condescend, you said.

TELLING. Christ, who is he? God?

MURPHY. He is not God. But he was in Derry. And through being in Derry, he came to the people. You were not in Derry.

TELLING. So I was not in Derry!

NADINE. He taught you everything you know.

TELLING. Bollocks!

NADINE. Don't use that talk. Not in my bar.

TELLING. He's your fellar. You are not objective.

NADINE. You were bloody illiterate.

TELLING. Was I!

HART. I was.

NADINE. And so was he.

TELLING. He raised my consciousness. But I was not illiterate. Not all fuckin' squaddies are illiterate.

EDEN. He's here!

TELLING. I have a right to make my position clear. That's all I'm after. Making my position clear.

HART. Here's here now, Colin.

TELLING. All right, he's here! He's fucking here . . .

He drinks. CADBURY, *in his Major's uniform, comes in, stooping slightly.*

RICE. Morning.

CADBURY. I have an ulcer. I am to lay off drink.

NADINE. Well, you can't say you haven't asked for it.

CADBURY. I hate the body. The bloody thing is dying even in the womb. *(He goes to a table, sits.* NADINE *brings an orange drink.)*

MURPHY. Moderation in all things.

NADINE. You treat your body right, and it'll do the same by you.

CADBURY. Unfortunately, that is not the case. There is a terrible injustice in constitutions. Not just political ones.

NADINE. It's like a car. It's like any bit of machinery.

RICE. *His* car! If his car's anything to go by, Christ . . .

TELLING. Can we talk business? Just a little bit?

CADBURY. The danger is that they can perforate. I would hate to perforate in the middle of parade. I imagine there is some frothing at the gob.

EDEN. Yer legs twitch. And you wet yerself.

HART. You would look a bloody fool.

TELLING. MICK IS DEAD.

CADBURY. They give you these vile tablets to chew . . .

He pops one in his mouth. Pause.

TELLING. What we are into is called treason. And the rap is very big for that.

CADBURY. Disembowelling.

TELLING. This fucking casual attitude. This is not an outing to the seaside, is it? Or is it? If it's a seaside outing I would like to know.

CADBURY. The more it resembles a seaside outing the happier I shall be.

TELLING. And that's your answer, is it? On Mick's dead body. That's your answer. *(Pause.)* Fucking funny conspiracy.

CADBURY. You have a thing about conspiracy.

TELLING. What are we, then? If we aren't a conspiracy?

CADBURY. We are the Democratic Movement of the Army.

TELLING. Well I say that's a fucking conspiracy!

CADBURY. As soon as we think of ourselves as one, we will become one. And then we will become a cell. Cells are private and exclusive. I am not in favour of cells and I am not in favour of exclusion.

TELLING. A subversive group must have a structure—

CADBURY. I hate this text-book phraseology! I am sick of the Soviet example and the Algerian example. Let us do this our way!

TELLING. Yeah. Open shop.

CADBURY. There is no such thing as secrecy. It is a myth.

TELLING. Well, what are we lurking here for, then? We should hold meetings in Trafalgar Square. Get the pigeons in on it!

MURPHY. Don't be bloody silly, Col.

TELLING. I am asking him a question. Are we telling every geezer who drops in here what this game is all about? Excuse me, what's this Democratic Movement of the Army I've been hearing all about? Oh, that. It's a body of officers and other ranks sworn to defend the working class and overthrow the government in the event of civil war, and we meet at 8 o'clock on Thursdays in the Oakleigh Arms. *(Pause.)* It's not a fucking darts match!

EDEN. Col has a point.

TELLING. I have a point.

They all look at CADBURY, *in anticipation. Suddenly* GODBER, *who has been sitting silently at the back, stands.*

GODBER. Like me. I could be anyone. Is that your point? *(They look at him.)* On my first day at school, I was informed that I was among the top two and a half per cent of England's brains. I calculated that this meant only two million people had what I had, and a lot of those were senile or the victims of disease. I was therefore a leader of society. It seemed obvious I would be rewarded appropriately. For example, I could own property. I could have a small estate. *(They laugh.)* However, when it came to leaving I discovered that I had been misled. Although I had the A levels, I was not invited to become a leader of society. I did not even have a job. *(They laugh.)* I discovered that the nation was in serious decline. It looked as though nobody would be able to own a small estate. It was obvious a new society was on the way. *(Pause.)* But then it dawned on me. Were we really ready for the new society? Because when I looked around me, although most people could never have a small estate, there were some people who still managed it. In spite of everything. They managed it. So how could that have come about? *(Pause.)* And then I knew that I was nobbled. From the cradle, they had nobbled me. And I will not be nobbled by the capitalists. *(Pause.)* For all you know, I am a spy. But where's a bloke to go if not here? How are we to find each other?

They look at him. He sits.

TELLING. Like the man says. For all we know he is a spy.

HART. Oh, come on, Col.

TELLING. We do not know!

Pause.

CADBURY. I never wanted us to end up in the stagnant backwaters of private politics. I have never seen us as a fervent little gang, dribbling theory over dog-eared paperbacks . . .

TELLING. No. You want a mass party, don't you? You want summer schools on a bleeding bishop's lawn. *(He drains his glass, gets up, belts his tunic.)*

CADBURY. A secret cell. Stuck to one another like a clip of cartridges. That would be a Special Branch man's dream.

TELLING *(going out)*. I wanna live. I'm funny like that. I dunno what's the matter with me. *(As he goes out he meets MCPHEE coming in.)*

MCPHEE. Excuse me, mate. I'm lookin' for a Major Cadbury.
(TELLING *looks at him, then at* CADBURY *with an expression
of supreme contempt. He goes out.)* Nice geezer. *(He goes to the
bar.)*
NADINE. Yes.
MCPHEE. I'll have half to kick off wi'. *(He looks around, sees*
CADBURY.) You would nae be Major Cadbury?
NADINE. Who told you he would be in here?
MCPHEE. Some feller.
NADINE. Who?
MCPHEE. Oh, Christ, I've noo idea.
NADINE. Where?
MCPHEE. In a pub.
NADINE. What pub?
MCPHEE. It's nae a crime to be in here! *(Pause. They all watch
him as he sips.)* He said too did nae care much for the govern-
ment. Noo more do I. Tha's all. *(Pause.)* He said this was the
place to go. If yoo were fucked off wi' the government. Tha's
all. *(Pause.)* He called yoo the governor.
CADBURY. Why don't you like the government?
MCPHEE. Well, tha's a big question. *(They look at him.)* There's
a whole lot of things, you know . . . *(He shifts uncomfortably.)*
I think they're bastards, if yoo wanna know.
CADBURY. What are you drinking?
MCPHEE. Bitter.
CADBURY *(to* NADINE). Can we have a pint of bitter?
MCPHEE. Tha's very kind of yoo.
CADBURY. About you and the government.
MCPHEE *(smiling).* Billy . . .
CADBURY. Billy. *(Pause.)* It's difficult to be specific. When you're
asked.
MCPHEE. It fuckin' is. Yoo know . . . there's so much . . . really
gets yoo . . . yoo could go on for hours . . . *(Pause.)* The things
they do. It's terrible.

HART *delivers the beer.* MCPHEE *gulps it with relief, stops.*

CADBURY. Finish it.
MCPHEE. Thank yoo.
CADBURY. Drink up.
MCPHEE. Wha's this?
CADBURY. Get it down you. Bottoms up.
MCPHEE *(with a bemused grin).* Okay. Yoo think I canna do it,
you're mistaken. *(He drains the glass.)*
CADBURY. Now stand up on that chair and say one thing you've
got against the government. (MCPHEE *looks from* CADBURY
to NADINE, *to the men at the bar.)* One thing. (MCPHEE
reluctantly climbs onto a chair.) One thing.

MCPHEE. I doon't . . . yoo doon't . . .

CADBURY. Any old thing.

MCPHEE. One thing . . . I doon't . . . Christ, I . . . *(He laughs weakly.)* I said I . . . Christ . . . ridiculous . . . there's so much I . . .

CADBURY. Get down.

MCPHEE. I'm nae at fuckin' school, I'm not!

CADBURY. Get down.

MCPHEE *(sudden inspiration).* Immigration!

HART. Get down!

MCPHEE. Immigration! There yoo are! Yoo asked. I said Immigration! *(He gets down slowly.)*

CADBURY. Now I'll say what *I* have against them. I have against them one shit on, trod down maggot of a life, hatched in the piss of poverty. I have against them one white worm's life of blind, bloody ignorance. I have YOU against them, doing your gutter scouring . . .

MCPHEE. Thank yoo for those few kind words. Yoo must take me for a fuckin' idiot.

CADBURY. I take you for a one-eyed shit dealer.

MCPHEE. Thank yoo.

CADBURY. I take you for gobbled-up mucus.

MCPHEE. Let me know when you've finished. I'm at the bar. *(He walks away.)*

CADBURY. Have you never had the longing to be a free man?

Pause. MCPHEE *turns to him.*

MCPHEE. A free man? An' what's a free man?

NADINE. If you don't know, then we can't tell yer.

MCPHEE *(turning to her).* I do not know! *(Pause.)* All this talk o' freedom. I ha' not had it. I ha' no even glimpsed it, an' the people I come from, they ha' nae glimpsed it either! *(He looks to* CADBURY.*)* Yoo ask me what a free man is, I tell yoo wha' a free man is. It is a man wi' a bellyful of grub, an' a room, an' a few quid in his pocket to go dancin' wi' the tarts with. Tha's what a free man is! The rest I do not know about, and do not even want to, for that matter. Yoo can keep the rest of it. To wipe your arses wi'. An' if yoo will nae serve me a drink, I'll go elsewhere. Will yoo serve me?

CADBURY. Have it on me.

MCPHEE. I'll pay mysel'. (NADINE *pours a drink.)* All this talk o' freedom. It is the nitter-natter of intellectuals.

CADBURY. It is privately owned. That is why you do not know what it is. It exists, but you are kept from it.

MCPHEE. Fuckin', sleepin', dressin' good, tha's freedom. Goin' to a great party wi' yer best mate and kippin' into Sunday, that's freedom. An' if yoo doon't know that', yoo don't know people.

(He takes the pint of beer, points to it.) Tha's freedom, mate. Cheers!
(He drinks, wipes his mouth.) Do I offend yoo? Do I cut yoo to
the quick? Do I hurt yoo wi' my fuckin' barbarity? *(Pause.)*
I make yoo creep. Yoo feel so fuckin' lonely when I am in the
room.

CADBURY. You have no idea of freedom. You have not even
caught a sniff of it.

MCPHEE. Who has it, then? Wha' I have never even sniffed?

CADBURY. The people you go running to. The people who pat
your head, you bassett-hound.

MCPHEE. Oh, so it is gin, is it? Not beer?

CADBURY. And even they don't have it.

MCPHEE. They don't have gin? They do have gin! I ha' seen 'em
drinkin' it!

CADBURY. Even they do not have freedom. They have privilege.
When they talk about freedom they are talking about privilege.

MCPHEE. Well, wha' in Christ's name is it, then? If they doon't
have it, and I doon't have it, who in fuck's name has it, then?
If it is neither beer, nor gin, nor fuckin' Campari for that matter,
wha' is it? I am dyin' to know, I am all ears! *(He stares hard at*
CADBURY.)

CADBURY. The English are afraid of it. It gives them agony. It
is like pissing bladder-stones . . .

Pause.

NADINE. They have set about the working classes! They are
putting the screws on your own people and you are helping 'em!

HART. That is all you need to know, sunshine.

EDEN. Kick their bollocks, or they will kick yours.

MCPHEE. I am sorry Mrs, I feel free. I do.

CADBURY. You are not. They have you. And you can't say no.
Freedom is saying no.

MCPHEE *hesitates, drinks deeply, looks around.*

GODBER. At this moment. *(They look at him.)* Later, freedom
will consist of saying yes. Is that not right?

MCPHEE *is confused.*

MCPHEE. I am sick of the word. I do not want to hear the word
again! *(He slams down the glass, goes out.)*

Blackout.

Scene Two

*A large window overlooking the Berkshire Downs. Seated in front of
it,* ORBISON *and* KNATCHBULL. GODBER *is standing to one side.*

KNATCHBULL.. This law is a good law. Sometimes when the
situation is dangerous you have to find another law. Or a better
way of reading the existing law. I think we have enough laws.
Except for this one. Because we must have powers, mustn't we?

ORBISON.   It will be exceptional law. Temporary and exceptional.

KNATCHBULL.   Naturally. Nobody likes extraordinary powers.
Except when the situation is extraordinary. And it is. It is getting
more extraordinary every minute. This power of arrest without the
nuisance of a trial is an extraordinary law. But for an extraordinary
situation. It is a law against mayhem. It is a law for civil war. Which
we have now, don't we? In a word. Though I hate to say it. We
must be frank.

ORBISON.   It is being described as fascist.

KNATCHBULL.   That word! That word! I would be, wouldn't it?
I think it is a sadly misused word. It has started creeping into
Hansard, I believe. With reference to yourself. And all of us . . .

ORBISON.   We are struggling to save a free society, as we know
it. Perhaps it is a notion that has no validity any more. Perhaps
we are the last of an epoch.

KNATCHBULL.   And they call that fascist! What a handy, empty word.

ORBISON.   Yes. But it hurts me.

KNATCHBULL.   It would do. You are a sensitive woman.

ORBISON.   History will be very hard on me. On all of us. But I am
not a fascist. I resent that very much.

KNATCHBULL.   You are not. You are most certainly not.

Pause.

ORBISON.   Let me tell you about this friend of mine. In Santiago
on a visit. Was walking along the street, a main thoroughfare,
well-lit, at Christmas time. People doing late night shopping,
buses, children, neon signs. And at the kerbside, four men
sitting in a massive car. This in a no-parking street, on yellow
lines. This one big car, with blanked-out number plates. With all
these traffic policemen, one illegally parked car, which as she
came abreast of it, started, mounted the pavement, two wheels
on the pavement, two wheels off, cruising beside her as she
walked, brushing her with the wing mirrors, she turning in
confusion to the policemen who refuse to notice her, or to people
who are scattering, cursing one another, thumping one another
with their gift-wrapped parcels in their scramble to escape. Until
at the corner, out they jump, four men in matching English
sportsman's caps, and fire bullets into her, into her back, and

legs, and thighs, into her neck and shoulders, and her heels and
feet, and as she lies there bleeding in the brilliant light of Woolworths,
Santiago, kneel beside her, actually kneel to fire into her nostrils,
in her ears, her eyes, her throat, her wrists and elbows, her belly, her
vagina and her knees, all this with the policemen still directing
traffic in the road . . . *(Pause.)* And the Minister, having this drawn
to his attention, denies it ever could have happened because it is
an offence to drive a car without the proper registration in his
country. *(Pause.)* That is fascism. And when people talk about
fascism in this country, I tell them that story.

Pause.

GODBER *(contemplating her).*   Her big arse, spread at its most
impressionable by a bout of teeneage horse-riding. Her big
knickers in plain white. Her leg hair. Her damp bra on Panorama.
Her warm tights with Robin Day. A woman fruity with the
menopause. A woman to make a queer vomit. *(Pause.)* And my
fingers, clamouring to fidget in her mush . . .

A second light comes on to KNATCHBULL *and* VERITY.

KNATCHBULL.   I wonder if we might leave it there, as Sweetheart's
been on her feet all day? Get in for Blue Peter and so on.
ORBISON.   Yes, of course. Only I'd like a word with Mr Godber.
On his own. Wait in the garden. Look around. (KNATCHBULL
looks at her with suspicion. They go out. ORBISON *looks
directly at* GODBER.) Do you lie and exaggerate?
GODBER.   You are so like you are on television . . .
ORBISON.   Do you lie and exaggerate? *(He still says nothing.)* On
the basis of your evidence I have just authorized the arrest of
Cadbury and the others. So I have to know if you are truthful. Do
you see? *(Pause.)* That is very simple, isn't it? Is it truthful?
About the stockpiling of rifles. I appeal to you.
GODBER.   It is truthful. And you do appeal to me. (ORBISON *is
horrified, stunned.* GODBER *gets up.)* Will you seduce me? Or shall
I seduce you?

She looks at him, appalled.

ORBISON.   My God.
GODBER.   You're shocked.
ORBISON.   I am not shocked.
GODBER.   You are shocked. You're shocked a man has said he finds
you sexually desirable.
ORBISON.   No, not for that.
GODBER.   Yes.
ORBISON.   No. It's the manner, it's—
GODBER.   The manner. The conventions.
ORBISON.   What the hell do you think you are?

GODBER. I fancy you. You thrill me. That is what you do to
me. What has the manner and the convention—
ORBISON. Will you go? Or do I have to get someone?
GODBER. The men you have. The little white mice of men you
have . . .
ORBISON. You are the victim of a silly, fashionable idea. The idea
that all men are wanted by all women, and all women by all men.
I do not want you. Not in secret, not in some thrilled, private corner
of me, not in the belly or the womb. Nowhere. *(Pause.)* Now please
go.

Pause, then he turns, goes out.

Scene Three

The garden is divided into two areas. In one area, KNATCHBULL *and*
VERITY *wait impatiently for* GODBER. VERITY *wanders a little
way.*

VERITY. We haven't got a garden.
KNATCHBULL. We've got a garden. It's a small one, but it is a
garden.
VERITY. It's a dump.
KNATCHBULL. It's small. I haven't given it all the attention I would
like.
VERITY. It's a dump.
KNATCHBULL. Don't say that again, Sweetheart.
VERITY. It's a dump.
KNATCHBULL. Thank you.
VERITY. She's got this great big garden. Why haven't we?
KNATCHBULL. Because it isn't ours. It's hers.
VERITY. Why?
KNATCHBULL. It isn't ours. That's all there is to it.
VERITY. That's not an answer.
KNATCHBULL. Have you seen Mr Godber?
VERITY. Answer it.
KNATCHBULL. Don't come it, Sweetheart.
VERITY. Answer it.
KNATCHBULL. Look, either you own things or you don't! It's like
blue eyes. Either you have them or you don't. It's like spina bifida,
either you get it or you don't! *(Pause.)* Where's Godber? Have you
seen Mr Godber? Sweetheart?

In the second area of the garden, GODBER *is walking across when a
tennis ball bounces past him. He catches it, is about to throw it back,
but stops.* RHODA *appears, in tennis clothes.*

RHODA. My ball.

GODBER. Yes.

RHODA. Can I have it.

GODBER. I have just tried to seduce your mother.

RHODA. I know you. Seedy Sam of the Serpentine.

GODBER. Seduce me instead.

RHODA *(holding a hand out for the ball).* Is that the best you can do?

GODBER. No time. Got to get back for Blue Peter.

RHODA. Sorry. It's 40-love and I'm serving very well.

GODBER. You can make it.

RHODA. I loathe your politics.

GODBER. I haven't got any.

RHODA. I loathe your lack of them. *(She extends her hand more deliberately.)*

GODBER. Stop thinking. Start to feel.

RHODA. Oh, not that old rubbish.

The lights go out on GODBER*'s area and rise on* KNATCHBULL*'s. The tennis ball bounces to them.* VERITY, *puzzled, catches it.*

KNATCHBULL. I used to ask myself these questions. I was always asking questions. And one question led to another, as they will. And in the end I was asking questions about everything—things I had never meant to question in the first place. I was going mad with it, as you are. I had question marks for eyeballs. *(Pause.)* And then I thought, this question-asking I'm engaged on is in no way making me happy. Quite the opposite. I thought of all the people who did not ask questions, and those who did. And it seemed the latter were less happy. And looking back to history, to Merry England and so on, you do not think of them as questioning, and yet it was obviously merry, wasn't it? I don't think it is a good idea to be calling into question everything. I think it's not a healthy state of mind. All right? *(Pause.)* I put it to you that way. About why this garden is not yours. It is not yours, all right? Just leave it there.

VERITY. I'll take this ball back, shall I?

KNATCHBULL. And ask for Mr Godber. *(He looks at his watch.)* Fuck it, we are in the rush hour!

Lights up on GODBER*'s area. He and* RHODA *are standing very close.*

RHODA. It may sound ridiculous, but I think there is something wrong with this. I actually think it is corrupt.

GODBER. Everything is corrupt.

RHODA. It isn't. Not everything. But it is corrupt to do something purely because your mother wouldn't. I know it is corrupt and I am still doing it.

Pause, then she puts her hand out to touch him. VERITY, *who has appeared with the ball, watches spellbound.*

VERITY. I touched his manhood. My heart was racing and my knees were weak. This was the moment I had been created for. I uttered an invul—an invul—an invol—untary little cry, oh do it to me now, my love!

Lights out on RHODA *and* GODBER.

KNATCHBULL. What I have now is the quality of serenity. I bow to the inevitable. I am a man who is going to make old bones. (VERITY *comes in.)* Found him?
VERITY. He is lying on top of a girl.
KNATCHBULL. Don't be clever.   .
VERITY. Her knees are up and he—
KNATCHBULL. CUT THAT OUT! Don't be silly. Let other children be silly. No need for you to be.
VERITY. You asked.
KNATCHBULL. I asked where Mr Godber was. I didn't ask for you to show off.
VERITY. You asked and I told you. He is lying on top of a girl.

KNATCHBULL *looks at her for a moment, then shoots out his hand.* VERITY *takes it and leads him out.* RHODA *is picking bits of grass from her tennis dress.*

GODBER. How often has that happened? Just like that?
RHODA. Never.
GODBER. Me neither.
RHODA. Well, well. *(She picks up her racquet.)* My serve.

She starts to go out. They are being watched by KNATCHBULL *and* VERITY.

GODBER. See me . . . !

She stops, then sarcastically.

RHODA. Don't spoil it.   .
GODBER. Spoil what?
RHODA. Exactly. *(She goes, calling.)* First service. Sorry.

GODBER, *sensing he is being watched, turns, sees* KNATCHBULL.

KNATCHBULL. Michael, I have to tell you this. I distrust you from the bottom of my heart.
GODBER. Why?
KNATCHBULL. Why. He asks me why.
VERITY. We're missing Blue Peter!
KNATCHBULL. You have such funny motives. You are most peculiar.
GODBER. I do my job.

KNATCHBULL. I think you are an idealist.

GODBER. No.

KNATCHBULL. I think you are pursuing something. I think you have a vision, Michael. And that bothers me.

GODBER. I'm my own man, if that's what you're driving at.

KNATCHBULL. No one is their own man. Not in this game.

GODBER. I am a cynic.

KNATCHBULL *(shaking his head)*. No.

GODBER. I am a cynic. Why don't you believe me?

KNATCHBULL. All this peculiarity on tennis lawns. You are an idealist of some description.

VERITY. We've missed Blue Peter, you pair of shits!

She stomps off angrily. KNATCHBULL *stares at* GODBER.

GODBER. Under all the stabbing and the torture you tend your little garden of good will. I tell you there are people WITH NO FAITH. Don't let your stinking optimism run away with you. Trust me.

Pause. KNATCHBULL *contemplates him.*

KNATCHBULL. I love your words. I think you string together lovely words . . .

Fade to black.

Scene Four

The Oakleigh Arms. NADINE *and* CADBURY *are sitting at a table.* MCPHEE *enters, stands uncomfortably for some time.*

NADINE. You came back then.

MCPHEE. I am no a moron. I will no have people think I am a moron. I have my pride.

NADINE. Take a seat then.

MCPHEE *(to* CADBURY*)*. If you don't abuse me. *(He sits nervously. Pause.)* Aboot me! *(Pause.)* I wanna knoo aboot myself. *(They look at him.)* Christ, help a geezer who comes here in good faith! *(Pause.)* Tell me!

NADINE. We won't tell you. If you want to, you tell us.

MCPHEE. I can't.

NADINE. Try.

MCPHEE. I can't! I canna talk!

CADBURY. You can describe yourself. Once you have a description of yourself, you're near to knowing why you fit it.

MCPHEE. You describe me. You tell me, please.

CADBURY. You don't want to know about yourself. You want phrases to cling to.

MCPHEE. Okay, I do!

CADBURY. You want to deliver yourself to the slogan.

MCPHEE. Okay! For starters that'll do!

CADBURY. I'm not your man, then. *(Pause.)* I won't tell you your life. Do not appeal to me. Appeal to nobody. No one can teach you what you do not know already. Do not let another man describe you. Describe yourself.

Pause, MCPHEE *gathers himself.*

MCPHEE. I went to school—

NADINE. Was born.

MCPHEE. I went to school—

NADINE. Why weren't you born?

MCPHEE. I was born, obviously . . . *(Pause.)* My father was a private in the Cameronians—

NADINE. That's it.

MCPHEE. He was a Corporal . . . I think . . . He was out in Africa . . . not when I knew him . . . then he was a Private—but he said at one time he had been a Corporal—

NADINE. Your mother.

MCPHEE. My mother?

NADINE. Yes.

MCPHEE. She was . . . she sometimes worked . . . she sometimes didn't . . . in a laundry . . . she had these hands . . . these fuckin' hands . . . because of the detergent . . . I will no forgive them—I could get indignant about that!

The lights go out on CADBURY *and* NADINE, *come up on* GODBER, *seated at a table eating.* MCPHEE *crosses the stage and joins him.*

GODBER. I'm expecting someone, Billy.

MCPHEE. When I first saw him, for wha' he called me, I cud ha' jammed a bottle in his face. Yoo saw me, I cud ha' carved the bastard, but noo I am full of respect for him. I ha' been very careless wi' respect. I ha' respected pop stars and fuckin' footballers, I ha' even respected blokes for fuckin' women, but I am havin' noo more of tha'. Now I respect mysel', an' yoo, and the Major. Tha's the lot.

GODBER. I am expecting somebody.

MCPHEE. As for the bastard Knatchbull—chop! I am a member of the Democratic Movement now.

GODBER. I see.

MCPHEE. I don't think yoo do see.

GODBER. Go easy, Billy.

MCPHEE. I don't think yoo fuckin' see at all.

GODBER. Don't shake your political perspiration over me!

Pause.

MCPHEE. All right, I'm sorry. I am sorry. *(He leans back, then urgently*

forward again.) Christ, mate, I ha' nae had an idea in my head until
today. I ha' got an idea noo an' I have to tell yoo. That is what a mate
is for!

GODBER.   You have an idea.

MCPHEE.   I have!

GODBER.   Good. I also have an idea.

MCPHEE.   Okay, yoo have. Yoo are fuckin' lucky. Yoo had a proper
education, yoo were nae the victim of a rulin' class conspiracy. But
I wanna tell yoo what it means to look at mysel' in the mirror an'
say, Billy, there are reasons yoo are the worm yoo are. To know tha'!
It's like a puppet seein' it's got strings!

GODBER.   The Major has cut ice with you.

MCPHEE.   I am breakin' out of my prison. An' yoo would do well to do
the same.

GODBER.   I am not in prison.

MCPHEE.   Yoo are in prison, but yoo do not know it!

GODBER.   Then I'm not in prison.

MCPHEE.   Christ, yoo are! We all are, if only we knew it. Can't yoo
see?

GODBER.   You have stuck your mouth to a cunt, Billy, and you're
all of a shiver . . . *(He gets up, to take his plate out.)*

MCPHEE.   My father, in Africa, during the war—

GODBER.   I am expecting someone—

MCPHEE.   Listen to me, will yoo! (GODBER *looks at him, sits again.)*
My father, in the army out in Kenya, walkin' wi' a mate one day, they
passed this house an' this woman, this white woman, comes runnin'
to 'em and says this black geezer, this gardener or whatever he was,
had chucked his shovel down and sworn at her somethin' terrible.
An' so they looked for him, and found him sittin' in the woodshed,
doin' nothin', sittin' there, an' he would nae come out, an' they said
go to the Mrs an' apologize and then get on wi' your fuckin' work.
But this black would nae move. He just sat there. So they picked
him up and beat him. They beat him wi' these fuckin' logs. An' he
went back to the Mrs and he got down on his knees an' begged
forgiveness, an' picked up his shovel an' went back to work. An this
woman said thank yoo to my dad, an' gave him an' his mate a lager
on the step, an' they pushed off well satisfied. And he told me years
after what a thrill he had got out of it, an' how it was the best day of
his life, puttin' the nigger in his place. The best day of his life! Christ,
if tha' had been the best day of his life! Ma poor ol' man! The scum
beatin' the scum. I'm nae a soft bastard, but I could cry when I
think it was the best day of his life . . .

GODBER.   You angel, disguised as a tartan yob . . .

MCPHEE.   If I could get yoo t'agree wi' me!

GODBER.   Have ME with YOU.

MCPHEE.   Together.

GODBER.   I'm sorry, Billy, I'm—

MCPHEE. Okay, yoo are expectin' somebody! This is more important
  than your somebody! (GODBER *looks at him.*) Are yoo tellin' me to
  piss off, then?
GODBER. It's a woman, Billy.
MCPHEE. A woman? A fuckin' woman? *(Pause.)* Does she mean somethin' to yoo, then? *(Pause.)* Christ, it is deadly serious, is it?
GODBER. You are treading on my toes . . .
MCPHEE. Is it?
GODBER. I have an interest. An interest your hairy presence would
  obliterate, that's all. *(Pause, then* MCPHEE *turns up his collar, goes
  out.* GODBER *picks up his plate.)* There have been women here.
  Not inordinately. Not in flocks. We fucked, sometimes because I
  pestered, sometimes not. A teacher with a gold tooth. A nurse. A
  foreign student of catering. I don't think I have ever said sincerely
  I will ring you as they left . . .

He carries the plate out. RHODA *comes in, wearing a mac.*

RHODA. Not on your nelly, I thought. Traipsing across London to
  some fifteen quid a week shared attic, squeezing past the Honda in
  the dismal hall. For what? A dirty mug of coffee and an afternoon
  in unaired sheets . . . (GODBER *returns.* RHODA *is looking at a
  fluid-filled milk bottle on the chair.)* What's that?
GODBER. Urine.
RHODA. Yours?
GODBER. It's a long way to the lavatory.
RHODA. You have made it cosy.
GODBER. When there is a crateful, I take it away in bulk. A whole
  week's bladdering.
RHODA *(looks coolly at him).* You don't shock me. I'm sorry, but
  you really don't. *(She picks up the bottle, puts it on the floor, sits.
  Long pause.)* They've arrested twenty-seven journalists. (GODBER
  ignores this.) That's today's big news. *(He is still silent.)* And a lot of
  academics are to be dismissed. That's tomorrow's.
GODBER. The music goes round and round.
RHODA. You couldn't care?
GODBER. Could you?
RHODA. I am appalled.
GODBER. Or thrilled. The Big Dipper goes out of control. Monsters
  break loose. Monsters widely believed to be extinct. *(Pause.)* You
  cleanly educated people. You end up fetishists for snot.
RHODA. This wouldn't be an erotic preamble?
GODBER. What else did you come for?
RHODA. I came because there were so many excellent reasons why I
  shouldn't. And I was sick to death of them.

Pause. GODBER *looks at her for a long time.*

GODBER. I have a theory about the Romans. Do you want to hear it? *(Pause.)* I think they became so Roman they got fed up with it. They developed a preference for being Goths. All those areas they had in their reason and humanity chalked off, all the secret rooms they had hung silk cords across, they wanted to run about and scream in. And they did.

Pause.

RHODA. When things were all right here, I was very keen on chaos. As a fire to be gone through, for a specific betterness the other side. But now we are in chaos I find . . . I just like chaos.

GODBER. Looking in the abyss. And if it makes you dizzy, well, it makes you dizzy . . . That is all you need to be a star . . . stand outside their decency . . .

RHODA. Their decency, their reasonableness—their CULTURE! *(Pause.)* At university—I was at university— we started a theatre and we had this show—this amazing show we took on tour—in which at one point we dragged a man from the front row—physically dragged him by his arms and legs—and robbed him in the middle of the stage. We are committing an offence, we said. We are robbing him. And they sat there, his friends, and he laughed very weakly, all embarrassed, while we actually mugged him and undressed him and actually roughed him up a bit. And then we shoved him back in his seat and chucked his clothes at him, and he sat there pulling on his trousers almost secretly in case the actors were DISTURBED! And when the show was over, they all clapped, including him, and we all waited for him to ask for his money back. But he didn't. He left the pigskin wallet with the money in. And I thought that was very, very decadent. I thought that was VILE, STINKING DECENCY on his part. I said we had to go on from there and actually maim someone. Do someone an injury. Really FUCK THEM UP a bit!

GODBER *watches her, bemused.*

GODBER. You university wits. With your funny little appetites . . .

Fade to black.

Scene Five

An urban cemetery. A funeral progressing towards a grave. The coffin is supported by EDEN, RICE, TELLING, CADBURY, MURPHY *and* HART. *Walking behind,* NADINE *and* MCPHEE.

CLERGYMAN. Man that is born of woman hath but a short time to live, and is full of misery. He cometh up and is cut down like a flower. He fleeth as it were a shadow and never continueth in one stay. In the midst of life we are in death. Of whom may we seek for succour but of Thee?

They arrive at the grave. The coffin is slowly lowered onto its supports.

TELLING. I'll make a speech.

CLERGYMAN. Earth to earth, ashes to ashes, dust to dust, in sure and certain hope of the resurrection to eternal life, through our Lord Jesus Christ.

TELLING. I'll make a speech.

CLERGYMAN *(indicating they should lift the ropes).* I heard a voice from Heaven saying unto me—

TELLING. MY SPEECH!

CADBURY. We do not need a speech.

TELLING. I'm speaking for him. As he can't speak. I'm speaking for him.

CADBURY. Get on with the funeral.

CLERGYMAN. Even so saith the spirit, for they rest from—

TELLING. THIS MAN—THIS MAN—

CLERGYMAN. Their labours. Now is Christ risen. For since by man came death—

TELLING. THIS SAVAGED MAN—THIS TORTURED MAN—

CLERGYMAN. By Man also came the resurrection of the dead—

TELLING. TORTURED BY WILD ANIMALS—

CADBURY. Don't contaminate this with your bloody romanticism, I beg you.

HART. Give over, Col.

TELLING. By God. By God. *(He looks around.)* So we are just letting him go, are we? We are just putting Mick away, like he was a normal corpse? Like he was an old age pensioner?

NADINE. Stuff it, Colin.

TELLING. Like he was an accident?

CADBURY. This is no time for heroics.

TELLING. It's not heroics, it's a speech!

CADBURY. You are after being a legend. You want to be a drunk's song. Show a little dignity.

TELLING. You and your dignity. You cannot run a revolution on your dignity!

An Army truck drives on, stops with a skid. KNATCHBULL *and* BLEACH *appear. The mourners see them, as does the* CLERGYMAN, *who recites the end of the oration at breakneck speed.*

CLERGYMAN. The grace of our lord Jesus Christ, the love of God— fellowship of the Holy spirit—be with us evermore—amen! *(Clutching his surplus, he hurtles away.)*

Pause.

CADBURY *is watching* KNATCHBULL.

CADBURY. All right, make your speech.
HART. We've gotta run for it.
MURPHY. Stick together.
HART. Run for it.
CADBURY *(to* TELLING). Make your speech.
EDEN. I'm dropping it.

He lets go his rope, careers offstage. NADINE *steps into his place.*

KNATCHBULL. And then there were six.
BLEACH. They look a load of silly tits.
KNATCHBULL. The box goes in the hole.
BLEACH. You put it in the hole, stupid.
TELLING. THIS MAN . . . THIS MAN . . . DUMPED ON THE
    COMMON WITH HIS TORTURED FLESH . . . CHUCKED OUT
    LIKE A MATTRESS OR A RUSTY BIKE . . . HAD LIFE . . .
    WAS HUMAN . . . LAUGHED AND JOKED—
KNATCHBULL. Oh, dear, oh, dear . . .
BLEACH. Embarrassing, embarrassing . . .
TELLING. PLAYED WITH CHILDREN, SPENT HIS SPARE TIME
    IN A YOUTH CLUB WITH KIDS WHO HAD EVEN LESS THAN
    HE HAD—
BLEACH. The tears are running down my cheeks . . .
KNATCHBULL. Have they never heard of Churchill? He could
    speak.
TELLING. BECAUSE HE WAS A GOOD MAN, BECAUSE HE
    CARED—CAN YOU HEAR ME? YOU BUM-LICKING COPPERS,
    CAN YOU HEAR?—HE IS DEAD BECAUSE HE CARED!
KNATCHBULL. And they want to run the country. They have
    aspirations to running England . . .
TELLING. A COMMON, FUCKING SQUADDIE TORTURED TO
    DEATH. YOU BASTARDS IN THE LORRY, REMEMBER THAT—
KNATCHBULL. Time to go in, I think before it gets any more
    embarrassing—

He makes a sign to the lorry. MILITARY POLICEMEN *surge over.*
HART *runs off.*

FIRST MP *(shouts).* Don't bother, son!
SECOND MP *(to the mourners).* In the lorry, in the lorry . . .
MURPHY. I am a civilian. You cannot take me. I am a civilian.
THIRD MP. Just get in the lorry.
KNATCHBULL *(pointing to* MCPHEE). Not him.
MCPHEE. Not me? Why not me?
KNATCHBULL. Silly.
MCPHEE. WHY NOT ME!
NADINE. Yeah . . . why not you, Billy?

MCPHEE. TAKE ME!

KNATCHBULL. Don't show off. You are getting too professional.

MCPHEE. I am wi' these people! Yoo know tha'! Yoo are a
fuckin' bastard to lay this on me!

CADBURY. White worm. White worm to the end.

MCPHEE. I swear to you! I swear it, Christ!

KNATCHBULL. Billy, this is all good stuff. Now shall we leave it?

TELLING. We will murder you. Nothing is certain in this life
except one thing. We will murder you.

KNATCHBULL. Oh, dear.

TELLING. MY OATH ON IT!

The MILITARY POLICEMEN *herd them away.* MCPHEE *turns to*
KNATCHBULL.

MCPHEE. Yoo had better put me wi' 'em! Christ, yoo had!

KNATCHBULL. How could I do that, Billy? You heard what he
said to you.

MCPHEE *(staggered)*. I am going to ruin yoo. I don't know how yet,
but I am going to ruin' yoo! (KNATCHBULL *looks at him
impassively.)* Do yoo hear me! I am threatening yoo!

KNATCHBULL. With what, Billy?

MCPHEE. I knoo so much. I am too fuckin' knowledgeable for
yoo. I am gonna talk and talk! I am goin' mad wi' talking!

KNATCHBULL. To who, Billy? Who will you talk to? Now they've
shut the papers down?

MCPHEE. It doon't matter. I still frighten yoo . . .

KNATCHBULL. Come, come . . .

MCPHEE. I will noo keep quiet! Yoo will have to murder me!

KNATCHBULL. Somebody will, no doubt. Somebody will.

MCPHEE. Oh, Mr fuckin' Knatchbull, I frighten yoo . . .

KNATCHBULL. Your life is one fucking great disaster Billy, from the
shag that made you to the day they plug your arse . . . *(Pause. Then*
MCPHEE *spits and goes out.* KNATCHBULL *looks at the discarded
coffin. He calls out.)* Come on, let's get shot of this!

ORBISON *comes in, stands for a moment unnoticed. He sees her,
turns.*

ORBISON. I thought that was excellent. A thoroughly mature piece
of—what do you call it?

KNATCHBULL. Arresting.

ORBISON. Arresting. Yes.

KNATCHBULL. There will be interrogation, obviously.

ORBISON. Obviously.

KNATCHBULL. In depth, though.

ORBISON. Yes, of course.

KNATCHBULL. Real depth. *(Pause. They look at one another.)*
I mean, you do want convictions.

ORBISON. Yes. But nothing nightmarish.

KNATCHBULL. No. More bad dream.

ORBISON. How bad?

KNATCHBULL. Tossing and turning sort of dream.

ORBISON. Mildly.

KNATCHBULL. Mildly rotten night, yes. *(Pause.)* The other thing is . . . *(He shifts uncomfortably.)* De-commissioning an agent.

ORBISON. Speak plain English, will you?

KNATCHBULL. No. I can't.

TWO COUNCIL EMPLOYEES *enter, begin shovelling earth over the coffin.)*

ORBISON. What were you saying?

KNATCHBULL. I wasn't saying.

ORBISON. What weren't you saying, then?

KNATCHBULL. I wasn't saying that we had a problem with an agent. A boy who has turned communist. A boy without friends or relations.

ORBISON. You mean you want to kill him?

KNATCHBULL. ME? I don't.

ORBISON. Not personally, but you want him killed.

KNATCHBULL. I hate this 'killed'.

ORBISON. KNOCKED OFF! MURDERED! PUT TO DEATH! *(The* COUNCIL EMPLOYEES *look up, slowly return to work.)* There is so much abstraction in this business. We have to get back to the personal pronoun. Stop hiding in the semantic wood . . .

KNATCHBULL. Can I do it, then? Can I?

She walks a little, turns desperately.

ORBISON. I HATE THIS SO MUCH!

KNATCHBULL. Me too. Me too.

ORBISON. One gets this poisonous longing to just get on with it and RULE. In a humane manner, but in person. Cut through the shit. I firmly believe that honesty and power are not compatible because the people one is ruling are themselves not honest. That is not pessimism or manicheism, it is a fact.

KNATCHBULL. I don't care for people any more than you. In the mass.

ORBISON. Every concept on which an aspiration has been centred has an inbuilt tendency towards corruption and I simply cannot bear that fact.

KNATCHBULL. Shall I or shan't I?

ORBISON. I could scream, I am in such despair. Real bloody biblical DESPAIR!

The COUNCIL EMPLOYEES *lean on their shovels, watching this. Pause.*

KNATCHBULL. I take it that means yes, does it?

ORBISON. But we carry on, stained as we are, muck-ridden as we are, us social democratic politicians in our rags of rotted promises, stinking of compromise, lousy with graft, because in the last analysis we are actually BETTER PEOPLE than the people posing the alternative. We are better people by the one criterion that really matters—the degree of suffering we inflict. In the scale of human misery we weigh very light. And I think we are purified by that. *(Pause.)* That is my opinion.

Pause.

KNATCHBULL. Thank you. Thank you very much.

He goes out, leaving her. Slow fade to black. ORBISON *doesn't move for a while.*

1ST COUNCIL EMPLOYEE. Don't I know yer face, Mrs.? *(She turns to them. He looks to his mate.)* Told yer. *(They both laugh nervously.)* He voted for yer. *(Pause.* 2ND COUNCIL EMPLOYEE *sniggers.)* I didn't. *(The* 2ND COUNCIL EMPLOYEE *sniggers again.)* I didn't vote. I've finished with voting. I have voted so often I am sick of it. I was digging when I first voted and I'm digging now. What has voting done for me? *(Pause. She looks at him with a small shake of her head, starts to go away.)* Tell me, then. *(She ignores him.)* Don't walk away! *(She goes out.)* Don't walk away you fucking bitch!

Blackout over their laughter.

Scene Six

A lane near the Devon coast. RHODA *and* GODBER *cycle on stage, stop, wait for* MCPHEE, *who arrives unsteadily. They all wear capes or macs.*

MCPHEE. Hang aboot, will yoo? I'm nae used to a fuckin' bicycle. *(He stops.)*

GODBER. Which way's the cottage, Billy?

MCPHEE. Every road's the same to me. Round and round in circles, hedges you canna see over. It's sheer fuckin' monotony.

RHODA. You are so urban. You are bricks and mortar, aren't you? To the marrow?

GODBER. Town rat is Billy. Fresh air's roasting his lungs.

MCPHEE. I wanna go back to London. No one will kill me. I don't believe I will be killed in London. Better than die of pneumonia in this dump.

RHODA. There's the lighthouse!

GODBER. You enjoyed the lighthouse . . .

MCPHEE. It is permanently drippin' in this place. Mists and
   clouds and fuckin' streams. I am sick of the sight of greenery.
   Wha's wrong wi' a park if you got to have some greenery?
GODBER. Somewhere that way there is an army camp.
RHODA. The sea is black. It is actually black. *(She stands stiffly
   and takes deep breaths.)*
MCPHEE. I do nae like the sea. If I liked the sea I wud ha' been
   a sailor. *(They breathe, ignoring him.)* Can we go back to London?
GODBER. Billy, there are people after your blood.
MCPHEE. We don't know tha'. How do we know? I cud be sittin'
   in London. I cud be safe as buggery.
GODBER. When someone tells you they are out to murder you,
   you have a choice. Either you believe them or you don't. But
   there are lots of bodies turning up in London. There is a real
   craze on for bodies, you know that. The Democratic Movement
   are into murder since the Major got put away.
MCPHEE. I will find 'em! I will tell 'em it was nae me that squealed
   on Cadbury!
RHODA. I think for a dosser, and a rapist, and an informer, and
   a junkie, and a rimmer, you are incredibly naive. That's what I
   think.
GODBER. You will go home. Have faith, Billy . . .

They prepare to cycle away.

MCPHEE. I am nae oblivious to gratitude. Yoo are a first class
   mate to bring me here. I never thought I'd end up wi' a mate
   like yoo.
GODBER. Billy, don't embarrass me . . .
MCPHEE *(preparing to ride).* I'll never get the hang of this.
RHODA. Cycling is like everything else, Billy. When you stop
   thinking, it is amazing what you can do.

She and GODBER *cycle away.* MCPHEE *gets comfortable and is
about to follow when two men in woollen face masks and army
great-coats freewheel across the stage, whistling tunelessly,* MCPHEE
stares after them, and wobbles off.

Scene Seven

A cottage in Devon. A wooden table and chairs. KNATCHBULL
and BLEACH *are sitting drinking from a flask.*

KNATCHBULL. Left Sweetheart at her auntie's. She sleeps with
   her cousin, in the same bed. Christ knows what they get up to.
BLEACH. Muck about under the sheets.
KNATCHBULL. Exploring one another's bodies, I shouldn't
   wonder.

BLEACH.   Infantile sex.

KNATCHBULL.   Quite natural. My wife I don't think knew a man's anatomy. Our wedding night was a scene of terror. I am all for Sweetheart having lots of physical relationships, trial marriages and so on. Film shows. Anything to stop a tragedy.

BLEACH.   Sex instruction.

KNATCHBULL.   Certainly.

BLEACH.   I read in the paper two instructors actually did it. With their clothes off. In front of six year olds. They got gaoled.

KNATCHBULL.   I would be happy for a kid of mine to see that.

BLEACH.   With the woman going—you know—making a noise?

KNATCHBULL.   They do, don't they?

BLEACH.   Some do.

KNATCHBULL.   Some do. And if they do, well that is—

BLEACH.   Not all of them.

KNATCHBULL.   Obviously. Not everybody makes a noise in farting do they? Some are silent, some are not.

BLEACH.   My point is—

KNATCHBULL.   I would be happy for the woman to let out a noise. *(Enter* GODBER, *removing his cape. He sees* KNATCHBULL *and* BLEACH. KNATCHBULL *looks up.)* With you, is he? *(*GODBER *removes his cape, provocatively silent.)* We have come a long way, Michael, haven't we? I hope he is here.

GODBER.   He gets behind, that's all. He is rotten with bicycles.

KNATCHBULL *stares at him, full of suspicion.*

BLEACH.   Did it in four hours. Thanks to the motorway. We were in Trafalgar Square at half past three.

Enter RHODA. *She looks amazed.*

KNATCHBULL.   Hope you don't mind. Us letting ourselves in. But we brought our own tea things, didn't we?

RHODA *(to* GODBER).   Are they—what are they—

GODBER.   Watch. Just watch.

RHODA.   I don't understand why they—

GODBER.   Or don't watch.

She looks at him, puzzled. Pause.

BLEACH.   To get back to the noise issue, it might give the impression—

KNATCHBULL.   It's real, isn't it? I'm all for reality.

BLEACH.   Kids might get the idea it was pain. That the woman was letting out. I think you would have to pick women instructors who were not too noisy, who made it very obvious that it was pleasure.

KNATCHBULL.   A noise of pleasure.

BLEACH.   Very clearly.

KNATCHBULL.   Make the noise, then.

BLEACH. Make the noise?

KNATCHBULL. The noise of pleasure you are on about.

BLEACH. Don't be stupid, I can't—

KNATCHBULL. You just said a noise of pleasure.

BLEACH. All right, a sort of hum.

KNATCHBULL. Well, do it.

BLEACH. I am not a woman, am I? How can I—

KNATCHBULL. You see, you people, all you want is to hide things. You are all for gilding the gingerbread. Kids are very realistic. You cannot deceive them by picking women who make a very special noise. The noise is almost certainly related to the man. He might make a bloody awful noise for all we know. What do you do then? It's a noisy business.

RHODA. I'm not staying.

GODBER. Sit down.

RHODA. This is vile.

KNATCHBULL. Oh, come on, darling. There is nothing vile about the human body. It is the one pure thing that I can think of.

RHODA. Oh, Christ. This man.

KNATCHBULL. Don't take my word for it. Look at the Greeks. They were nuts about naked flesh. That's why they painted it on jars. Any old pots they stuck the human body on. I'm sorry if I embarrass you.

RHODA. YOU DO EMBARRASS ME!

MCPHEE *comes in, stops, surprised.* BLEACH, *his hand in his pocket, rises to his feet.*

KNATCHBULL. Don't make a break, Billy. Don't make a run for it.

MCPHEE *is motionless, staring at* GODBER.

GODBER. When you're a star, nobody asks you to apologise for your act. No Bay City Roller ever got upset when he hit old women with his Mustang. Keith Moon didn't weep when he reversed over his chauffeur. It's all blood to the erection, Billy. It's all tinsel to the act.

Pause. MCPHEE *is still.*

KNATCHBULL. I don't think I ever got the hang of you Michael, did I? Ever get the hang of you?

GODBER. The gas has been turned up Billy, and we are boiling over . . .

KNATCHBULL. Having a daughter, I despair. Looking at Michael here, I despair. To think the world contains such people. You think you reach the bottom, but there is even lower. Michael, you shock me.

BLEACH. Well done lad.

KNATCHBULL.   No, I said he shocks me. He does. *(Pause.*
MCPHEE's eyes are still on GODBER.*)* I think people are
deteriorating. If you look at history there have been times when
people seemed to sink down very low. I think this must be one
of them. *(Pause.)* I'm sorry, Billy, it must be the situation, you
see. That's to blame for your situation . . .

Pause, then RHODA, *in a shock of disbelief, goes to* MCPHEE, *stands
inches from his face.*

RHODA.   Scream. *(Pause.)* They want to kill you. SCREAM!
(Pause.) Don't just stand there you fucking Auschwitz Jew!
(Pause.) Christ, this stinking PASSIVITY!

She slaps him in the face. KNATCHBULL *jumps to his feet.*

KNATCHBULL.   No call for that! Don't dare to do that. I hate that!
RHODA.   I am here! What about me! I am here! *(She looks to*
KNATCHBULL *and* GODBER.*)*
KNATCHBULL.   Yes, well so you are.
RHODA.   My mother. I have my mother. Are you mad? My MOTHER!
KNATCHBULL.   Oh yes, her.
RHODA.   Doesn't that mean anything to you?
KNATCHBULL.   I think we've moved on. Since that might have
meant anything to me . . . *(He looks at her.)*

Suddenly MCPHEE *begins singing.*

MCPHEE.   'This could be the last time, This could be the last time,
It may be the last time, I don't know . . . '

MCPHEE *bursts out laughing.* KNATCHBULL *buttons his coat.*

KNATCHBULL.   Not far to the beach, is it? Could come here for
the holidays.
MCPHEE *(grinning.)*   Are we goin' to the beach?
KNATCHBULL.   That's right.
MCPHEE.   Nude bathing. Sex in the moonlight!
KNATCHBULL.   That's the kind of thing. All right?

They move towards the door. MCPHEE *turns to* GODBER *and*
RHODA.

MCPHEE.   Yoo're nae comin'?
GODBER.   We're not coming.
MCPHEE *(with a leer).*   Just me an' them.

Pause, then he follows KNATCHBULL *and* BLEACH *out. For a
long time* GODBER *and* RHODA *remain silent, in their places.
At last, she looks up to him.*

RHODA.   If you can sit there when that is happening . . . if you
can watch and not do anything . . . you are finished, aren't you?
You are done.

GODBER *smiles. He reaches out his hand to her. Suddenly, the two figures in woollen face masks rush on and cover both her and* GODBER's *heads with sacks. They then shoot them through the sacks. The bodies slump to the floor.*

CYCLISTS *(in unison).*   The Sentence of the Court of the Democratic Movement is death. Have you anything to say?

As the lights dim on this, the flashing of the lighthouse becomes apparent.

Scene Eight

The beach at night. The five second flash of the lighthouse sweeps the stage. Slowly, staggering from the extreme depth of the stage, naked and half-drowned, MCPHEE *appears. He staggers to the front, opens his mouth to speak, but nothing comes out.*

MCPHEE.   I . . . *(He swallows, pauses.)* I . . . *(He hesitates, gaping. Slowly, a smile of relief crosses his face.)* I. *(He begins to laugh, holding himself in his arms.)* I! I! *(He rolls about on his knees in ecstasy.)* I! I! I!

The lights fade on him yelling. The lighthouse flashes.

THE END

Credentials of a Sympathizer was commissioned by BBC Television and first performed in the season 'Plays Television Would Not Do' at the RSC's Warehouse Theatre on February 21st, 1979.

The cast were:

GILDERSLEEVE	Edward Jewesbury
AMBER	Nicholas Le Prevost
GLAZING	Iain Mitchell
HACKER	Christopher Benjamin
CLOUT	Roderick Smith
SERGEANT ROYCE	Ron Cook
PRIVATE MILLER	Peter Hugo-Daly
TULLY	Charles Wegner
DUCKER	Philip Dunbar
MORAHAN	Michael Bertenshaw
EDEN	Tony McHale
FRASER	Christian Burgess
SIMS	Anthony Kane
WOMAN JOURNALIST	Fleur Chandler

Stage Directions read by Terence Harvey
Directed by Barry Kyle

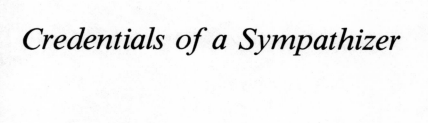

Credentials of a Sympathizer

Scene One

An empty hall, large and functional. It is dirty and decayed. The more utilitarian it appears, the better. Heating pipes and radiators. A clerestory window.

During the blackout, noise of voices and dragging of chains and bolts across padlocked doors, which at last swing back.

VOICE. Lights! Lights!

The theatre is lit. A cluster of people are standing in the doorway. Curiously, they nose forward, careful to remain behind GILDERSLEEVE, an immaculate man in hat and gloves. Either side of him, similarly dressed, AMBER and GLAZING. Behind them, HACKER, in trilby hat and CLOUT, his assistant, in overalls. Behind them, an army sergeant and two private soldiers. Bringing up the rear, with mops and buckets, TWO LADY CLEANERS and TWO REMOVAL MEN.

The group shuffles into the middle of the room, looking about them. Silence but for footfalls and the clanging of buckets. They look to GILDERSLEEVE enquiringly. Pause.

GILDERSLEEVE. Get it spick. (AMBER *nods seriously.)*
When they talk about it, let them say the place was spick.

Pause, then he turns and goes out, the group parting to make way for him. He is followed by AMBER and GLAZING. Pause, until they have gone, then an instant hum of chatter.

HACKER *(clapping his hands).* All right ladies! At your
leisure! *(The group breaks up.)* Correction! Not at your leisure,
in your very best time, please!

The LADY CLEANERS *begin working across the floor. The* REMOVAL
MEN *lounge in a corner, hands in their pockets.*

CLOUT. Tables Mr Hacker? Do we want the tables in?
HACKER. The floor first, Clout. When the floor is excellent—
then the tables.
CLOUT. And the winders?
HACKER *(looking up at the clerestory).* I note the winders.
Someone will have to do those, Christ knows how . . . *(They
both gaze up.)* How *do* they clean those winders?

63

PRIVATE MILLER. Shoot 'em out.

HACKER *(sarcastically)*.   That's wonderful.

PRIVATE MILLER.   Six rounds rapid.

HACKER.   Thank you. I'll bear than in mind.

PRIVATE MILLER *(drifting away)*.   Say the word . . .

HACKER.   Clout, are there ladders?

CLOUT.   Step ladders.

Pause.

HACKER.   Then that's our weak point. Winders in clerestory.
Right? *(He jots it down in a dog-eared notebook.)* Time is the
enemy. *(He looks to the* CLEANERS.*)* Ladies, can we buck
it up a bit? *(They look at him).* Back Britain for a change, eh,
darlings?*(He looks to the removers.)* Is the van outside, gents?
(One nods.) Backed up? *(Nods again.)* Outside the door? *(And
again.* HACKER *turns back to* CLOUT.*)* That staircase is a
bloody disaster. Have you measured it?

CLOUT.   Three foot two inches.

HACKER.   Christ, that's narrer.

CLOUT.   Three turns.

HACKER.   That's a bugger. *(He strokes his chin anxiously.)*
That is a bugger. *(Pause, then he looks to the* REMOVERS.*)*
Do you wanna make a start then, gents? *(They shrug.)* If you
would please. Thank you. *(They go out. He addresses* CLOUT.*)*
Pile 'em in the corner till the floor's done. And the chairs.
Stack 'em, this end, until they've finished. Christ knows when
that'll be, the way they move. *(He claps his hands at the women.)*
Come on, please girls, you're in the Common Market now! *(He
looks back to* CLOUT.*)* Have you got the seating plan? (CLOUT *nods.)*
Okay. But don't rush anything. Nothing to be overlooked. No
skimping on this one, okay? (CLOUT *nods.* HACKER *beckons him
closer.)* This has got to look good, Clout, I mean that. These are
our credentials. Seize the time, all right?

CLOUT.   Mr Hacker.

CLOUT *goes to supervise the* REMOVAL MEN. HACKER *wanders
anxiously around, looking at his watch. He stands near the soldiers,
leaning on the wall.*

PRIVATE MILLER *(mocking his nervousness).*   'Fe—ver . . .
Got fe—ver . . .'

HACKER *looks at him.* MILLER *grins.*

Scene Two

\ trestle table. A bench. Some wooden chairs. Sitting before a small portable mirror, GILDERSLEEVE *is shaving.* AMBER *is brushing his suit.*

GILDERSLEEVE. I was in a Non-Smoker. *(He draws the razor neatly through the soap.)* Coming up from Portsmouth. And this gang of louts got in. Five seconds, I thought, and they'll be lighting up. *(He cuts another swathe.)* I got to three. You know how I feel about tobacco.
AMBER. Quite.

GILDERSLEEVE *dabs his chin.*

GILDERSLEEVE. So I fetched the guard. And he told them to put their cigarettes out—if they wouldn't mind, if it wasn't too much trouble. He was all apologies to these louts. *(He shaves.)* But they gave him lip. *(Again.)* And I noticed this guard was slovenly. Like a refugee to look at. All creases and no tie. He had a tartan shirt, I think. *(He mixes more soap.)* After some futile recrimination, the guard withdrew. And they chucked insults after him. *(He takes up the razor.)* I looked lumbered with their stale tobacco all the way to Waterloo. *(He shaves.)* And then the ticket inspector appeared. Starched collar, small tie knot, neat as a bumble bee, pink with fresh shaving. An immaculate inspector with a carnation in his buttonhole. *(Pause. He recollects fondly.)* Gentlemen. This is a No—Smoking compartment. *(He looks to* AMBER.*)* Like sheep, they stubbed their stinking fagends on the floor.
AMBER. Good. Very good!

GILDERSLEEVE *wipes his face, gets up, throws aside the towel.* GLAZING *folds it.*

GILDERSLEEVE. Did we bring the Trinity tie?
AMBER *(holding out a tie.)* Coldstreams.
GILDERSLEEVE. Would they spot that? Are they *au fait* with regimental ties?
AMBER. They know cap badges. When they shoot a soldier they invariably get the regiment.
GILDERSLEEVE. Yes, but not the ties?
AMBER. I doubt it.
GILDERSLEEVE. Not the ties, surely.
AMBER. No.

AMBER *watches* GILDERSLEEVE *tie a masterly knot.*

GILDERSLEEVE.   Vital. Being here first like this. Being
  in occupation. Appearing like star actors from our dressing
  room. And them all creased and sweaty from their car.
  *(He takes two hairbrushes, sweeps back from his
  temples.)*

Scene Three

CLEANERS *are moving steadily across the hall. The* REMOVAL
MEN *are bringing in a table.* CLOUT *piles chairs. The soldiers
lounge.*

PRIVATE ROSE.   When you think how all the great wars ended . . .
  the railway coach at Compiegnes . . . the tent at Luneburg . . .
  MacArthur at Panjomong . . . *(He looks at* HACKER, *who is
  dusting ledges with a feather duster.)* This becomes us very
  well . . .
HACKER.   CLOUT! *(He jerks his head.)* Over here!
CLOUT *(scurrying)*.   Mr Hacker?
HACKER.   Is the catering here?
CLOUT.   Not to my knowledge.
HACKER.   NOT TO YOUR KNOWLEDGE . . .!
CLOUT   It isn't, no.
HACKER   Bloody hell . . . *(He wipes his mouth.)* Are all the tables
  here?
CLOUT   Six, yes.
HACKER   Bloody miracle. And the coverings?
CLOUT   In the van.

HACKER *thrusts the feather duster at* CLOUT, *goes out.*

SERGEANT ROYCE *(contemplating the activity)*.   History this,
  ain't it? History in the making.
PRIVATE ROSE.   I've been on Panorama. Were you on Panorama,
  Malc?
SERGEANT ROYCE.   'Death of a Soldier'?
PRIVATE ROSE.   No. 'One Dark Night'.
SERGEANT ROYCE.   Nope.
PRIVATE ROSE.   After my wound stripe.
SERGEANT ROYCE.   Missed it. Sorry.
PRIVATE ROSE.   What are your feelings after you've been hit? He
  asked me. Geezer from the BBC. *(Pause.)* It was cut out. My
  feelings after I'd been hit.

PRIVATE MILLER. I hate fiascos. I hate seeing our flag
dragged in the muck. Talking to these bastards we've been
shooting at.

SERGEANT ROYCE. In ten minutes. Up them steps. Our
little bit of history.

PRIVATE MILLER. Our top knobs, talking to them . . .

PRIVATE ROSE. In this unlikely hole. Not even boy
scouts would wanna DYB DYB DYB in here.

HACKER *comes in with the last of the tables and* THE REMOVAL
MEN.

HACKER. *Vis-à-Vis* the tables, gentlemen, the arrangement of
the same must be in accordance with this plan. *(He waves a
paper.)* This strict plan. No deviations, please. Unto the inch.
Heed Mr Clout. *(He turns to* CLOUT, *gives him the paper.)*
On your head be it, Clout. Have you got the tape measure?

CLOUT. Mr Hacker.

HACKER. I shall have to trust you. I must put my faith in
you. Unto the inch. *(He goes out.)*

PRIVATE MILLER. This plan, this STRICT plan is at the
dictate of murderers. This slum, chosen by them. Touching our
caps, Lord Murderers.

SERGEANT ROYCE. They drew a line between our headquarters
and their headquarters, and then bissected it. And then
they chose the nearest hall. Half an hour to get
ready.

PRIVATE ROSE. Using a compass it should be possible to
work out where their HQ is. I wonder if they thought of
that?

SERGEANT ROYCE. Intelligence is up to all them tricks.

PRIVATE MILLER. Could pounce. Could leap on 'em.

PRIVATE ROSE. What? When they have flown this big nob
from Whitehall?

SERGEANT ROYCE. This here—this ceasefire—has priority.

PRIVATE MILLER. To have them sitting at a table, they would
suck their bums. To hear their voices they would piss
on our dead mates . . . The PATRIOTS . . .

Scene Four

A telephone on the staircase. Spot on HACKER.

HACKER. Hacker. Junk specialist, with his rat-infested
warehouse. By appointment to Her Majesty! My tender so low
as to be embarrassing. So low as to represent an actuarial loss.
And the opposition very scanty, because in this district

there aren't many even in possession of equipment for a garden
party, sitting down being a rarity round here since the troubles . . .
(He grins.) Well snatched, you grabber of good opportunities . . .
(He pushes a coin into the telephone.) Hello? *(He thumps into the
box.)* Sod it! Hello? Is that you, Frank? *(Pause.)* Hacker. HACKER!
(Pause.) About those tea-urns, Frank . . . TEA-URNS . . . *(Pause.)*
Have you got the wireless on? *(Pause.)* TEA URNS NO HAVE
ARRIVED. *(Pause.)* Christ, Frank—I must have support, Frank!
(Pause.) All right . . . all right . . . all right . . . all right . . .

Fade spot.

Scene Five

AMBER *and* GLAZING, *fully prepared with papers under their arms.
Pause. Sound of a lavatory not flushing, and many efforts. At last*
GILDERSLEEVE *appears.*

GILDERSLEEVE.   No flush *(He rolls down his sleeves,* GLAZING
   holds out his jacket.) Cracked hand basin.
GLAZING.   Doesn't it make you think of weddings? I always think
   of weddings.
AMBER.   Best man hovering in the vestry.
GILDERSLEEVE.   Will they wear black suits?
GLAZING.   Like a Holy Synod.
GILDERSLEEVE.   Surely they won't wear their hoods? Or dark
   glasses? I want to see their faces. I can't talk if I can't see
   their faces.
GLAZING.   We've cleared that. Normal faces will be worn.
GILDERSLEEVE.   Like the Inquisition otherwise. Difficult to take a
   team of wizards seriously.
AMBER.   By the way, there was a shooting. While you were in the
   lavatory. No details. Nor of casualties.

GLAZING *brushes the shoulders of his jacket.*

GILDERSLEEVE.   A big one, I imagine. To set us off. No point in
   trivial woundings at this stage.
AMBER.   Quite.
GILDERSLEEVE.   In celebration. Popping the red champagne.
AMBER.   Will they be armed?
GILDERSLEEVE.   We can't have that.
AMBER.   Three of them. To match our soldiers.
GILDERSLEEVE.   But out of sight? I won't have firearms
   visible.

GLAZING. That's been cleared.

GILDERSLEEVE. That's in the contract?

GLAZING. No it's agreed.

GILDERSLEEVE. But written down?

GLAZING. No. Nothing's written down.

AMBER. It's verbal, sir.

GLAZING. There are no documents as such.

GILDERSLEEVE. I see. *(He gets up, takes a final look at himself.)* How long have we got?

AMBER. Ten minutes.

GILDERSLEEVE. They'll be on time. They think it'll impress us how steely and efficient they can be. I despise promptness personally.

GLAZING. Did you know Mussolini had eight clocks in his limousine?

GILDERSLEEVE. Promptness is the supreme sign of lack of self-confidence.

GLAZING. Absolutely, I'm always early if I meet a girl. I'm afraid she'll go away otherwise. So what I do is perch somewhere near the rendezvous and watch for her. Then when she's been there five minutes or so, I swoop down, very casually. *(He grins.)*

GILDERSLEEVE. I hope you stuffed yourselves at lunch, I did.

AMBER. Roast baby duckling.

GILDERSLEEVE. I wasn't hungry but I was determined not to rumble. I shan't be picking at refreshments. In fact I think we might all abstain from biscuits. Let them pick. It's good psychology.

AMBER. Quite.

GILDERSLEEVE. So eat now if you must. Then clean your teeth. *(He goes out.)*

GLAZING *unwraps a bar of chocolate.*

GLAZING. I was thinking we could be back in London before six. All being well. Is that likely, do you think?

AMBER. Haven't the foggiest.

GLAZING. No, but I mean—does he dither?

AMBER. He is thorough.

GLAZING. But not finickity? Is he finickity?

AMBER. This ceasefire could save a lot of lives. I think he has every right to be finickity. (GLAZING *just looks at him.)* Sorry, but I believe that. *(He picks up some papers.)*

GLAZING. Ever been stock car racing?

AMBER. No.

GLAZING.   Class 1 speed trials. White City. Half past eight
   tonight. That's why I asked if he was finickity. *(He grins.)*

Blackout.

Scene Six

The hall. CLOUT *is kneeling on the floor with a tape measure, the
seating plan beside him. The* CLEANERS *have finished and are dusting.
Two* REMOVAL MEN *hold a table suspended.*

CLOUT.   Front legs here . . . on this spot here . . .
1ST REMOVAL MAN.   Okay . . . down . . .
CLOUT.   Couple of inches to the left, gents, please . . .
1ST REMOVAL MAN.   *(Staggering).* All right?
CLOUT.   Inch and a half . . .

They manoeuvre.

2ND REMOVAL MAN.   Whoa!
CLOUT.   Back a bit . . . beg pardon . . . back a bit . . . that's it.
   DOWN.
1ST REMOVAL MAN.   Down . . . Down . . .

The table is lowered. CLOUT *jumps up.*

CLOUT.   Four chairs . . . along here . . .

GILDERSLEEVE *comes in, wanders among the workers.*

SERGEANT ROYCE.   History on his shoulders. Saddled with history,
   poor sod.
PRIVATE MILLER.   From London, fresh as a daisy, crisp in his
   cellophane. Half an hour in this slum, then back there,
   kipping in his lovely sheets. And us blokes in the rain, behind
   our tin shutters . . .
GILDERSLEEVE *(Looking to them).*   You chaps all right?
PRIVATE MILLER.   ⎫
                                    ⎬ Sir.
SERGEANT ROYCE.   ⎭
GILDERSLEEVE *(looking at their rifles).*   Mustn't have those
   things in here . . .
SERGEANT ROYCE.   Sir.

The doors open. Enter two ladies clutching tea-urns.

1ST CATERER.   CATERERS!
CLOUT *(kneeling beside another table).*   Hold it ladies, if
   you don't mind, just one minute . . .

1ST CATERER. Hold it, he says.

CLOUT *(to the* REMOVAL MEN*)*. Down gents, where my finger is.

GILDERSLEEVE *(going to the door)*. *Two* tea urns?

HACKER *(pushing through with a huge trayful of pastries and a tube of plastic cups)*. Over there, ladies . . . the far wall please . . . *(He notices* GILDERSLEEVE.*)* Sorry . . . running very close to the wind . . . (HACKER *puts his load down.)* Down here, along this table . . . water's in the basement . . . *(He trips over* CLOUT *who is winding in his tape.)* Christ, Clout, nearly had me over! How are those chairs? *(He turns to the* CATERERS.*)* Unpack this lot, but go easy with 'em. Paper cups cost money, contrary to popular belief.

As the CATERERS *set up the refreshments,* GLAZING *and* AMBER *come in.* AMBER *goes direct to* GILDERSLEEVE.

GILDERSLEEVE. Who is the man in the trilby? The moustache and the trilby? Who's he?

AMBER. That's the furnisher, Hacker, sir.

GILDERSLEEVE. Our man?

AMBER. Certainly, sir.

GILDERSLEEVE. I have no confidence in him.

GLAZING *(joining them)*. His was the lowest tender, sir. By a long chalk.

GILDERSLEEVE. Are there no other considerations?

GLAZING. It's the way we operate, sir.

GILDERSLEEVE. I want to be in occupation! When they arrive. Sitting there.

AMBER. Two minutes yet.

GILDERSLEEVE. There are vast quantities of cakes over there. No one is to touch them. Is that clear?

AMBER. ⎫
⎬ Sir.
GLAZING. ⎭

GILDERSLEEVE. We mustn't keep them waiting. It's egg on our faces if we keep them waiting.

AMBER. Shall I take your right-hand side?

GILDERSLEEVE. Thank you.

Pause, as the final touches are put to the arrangements. HACKER *spreads a Union Jack across one row of tables. The others, facing from about five yards, are bare.*

AMBER. Terrifically like a wedding, sir.

GILDERSLEEVE. Nervous, Amber?

AMBER. Yes. When you think what this could mean.

GILDERSLEEVE. To your career?

AMBER. In people being saved. Lives spared and so on.

GILDERSLEEVE. That is not out business. That doesn't enter into it.
(Pause. AMBER *looks at him.)* Winning is our business. Winning
the ceasefire. Raking them into politics.

AMBER. Yes.

GILDERSLEEVE. Keeping their bloody fingers on the baize. *(Pause.)*
Right. Into our traps.

They go to the table. GILDERSLEEVE *sits in the middle,* AMBER
and GLAZING *on either side.* GLAZING *lays papers in front of
them.* HACKER *is busy putting up a blackboard and easel which
has a large urban map pinned to it.* CLOUT *puts finishing touches
here and there. The* CATERERS *withdraw. The soldiers stand at
ease by the doors.* HACKER *is about to leave but goes back and
polishes a place on the board moistening his handkerchief with his
tongue.* AMBER *and* GLAZING *sort and pass papers.*

AMBER. Did you ask for a cushion?

GILDERSLEEVE. No.

AMBER. I wish I had.

GILDERSLEEVE. Have you got piles?

AMBER. I think so. Yes.

GILDERSLEEVE. Mustn't get dependent on soft cushions. They
don't appreciate it. *(He turns in his chair to* GLAZING.)
How will we know they're coming up?

GLAZING. One of the soldiers— (GILDERSLEEVE *nods, turns
back.)* They're late.

AMBER. Very slightly behind time, yes.

GILDERSLEEVE   *(To* GLAZING *again.)* I'll want to break at
four fifteen.

GLAZING *nods.* SERGEANT ROYCE *comes in.*

SERGEANT ROYCE. The Gentlemen, sir.

Murmuring comes from the stairs outside. GILDERSLEEVE
and his men stand. GILDERSLEEVE *catches a glimpse of the
clerestory, still dirty.*

GILDERSLEEVE. Not spick. Those windows. Far from spick.

The murmurs get louder.

PRIVATE MILLER. If their shoulders touch me . . . if they brush me
me . . . I don't flinch. I have shot your sons, you bastards. And
you, the limping one, I hope it was my FN took a little piece
of you . . .

TULLY, DUCKER, MORAHAN *enter, stop just in the door.*

TULLY. Should there be refreshments, gentlemen, just take
the tea. Don't peck. We're not after charity.

They come right into the room.

GILDERSLEEVE.   Good afternoon, gentlemen.

Pause. They are looking at the jack.

TULLY.   We can't talk with that there.
GILDERSLEEVE.   I'm sorry, I—
TULLY.   The flag. Not talking to the bloody flag.

Pause. GILDERSLEEVE *turns to* GLAZING.

GLAZING.   Sir?
GILDERSLEEVE.   This flag.
GLAZING.   It's customary.
GILDERSLEEVE.   Is it?
GLAZING.   Sir.
GILDERSLEEVE *(perplexed). Is* it? *(He looks back to* TULLY.)
TULLY.   We're wasting time.
GILDERSLEEVE.   I'm afraid the flag is a normal feature of—
TULLY.   Then we don't talk

Pause, then GILDERSLEEVE *looks again to* GLAZING.

GLAZING.   Sir?
GILDERSLEEVE.   Early for a concession.
GLAZING.   Quite.

Pause, then with resolution.

GILDERSLEEVE.   Do it neatly. Fold it properly. With a
   touch of ceremony. Do not hurry it.
GLAZING.   Sir.
GILDERSLEEVE.   Whatever you do, don't humble it. *(He
   looks back to* TULLY.) Although it's normal practice for
   the Jack to be displayed—
TULLY.   This is not a normal meeting—
GILDERSLEEVE.   If I might finish— *(Deliberate pause.)*
   Although it's normal practice, I will in this instance,
   exercise my powers to waive this particular tradition.
   (Pause.) Remove it please.

GLAZING *and* AMBER, *with studied decorum go forward
and take up the flag. As they do so, the terrorist
representatives file into their places opposite. The flag is held
like a sheet, then* AMBER *and* GLAZING *join ends. It is
cleanly done. They return to their seats*

GILDERSLEEVE.   No skin off our noses. It's good to make
   concessions. On condition they are piddling.
TULLY.   What do they care for their flag? All they use it for
   is wrapping their corpses in.

He looks at GILDERSLEEVE *who is resting his chin on his fingertips. Pause.* GILDERSLEEVE *rises to his feet.*

GILDERSLEEVE. As I understand it, the conditions you are seeking as a basis for a ceasefire are as follows: one, complete withdrawal of the forces of the Crown to those positions occupied by them as at fifteenth December 19— *(He stops, his fingers poised around his spectacles.)*

TULLY. His style . . . his style is all of him . . .

Blackout.

Scene Seven

Two leather chairs, as in a TV studio. In one, a WOMAN JOURNALIST. *In the other,* TULLY, *legs spread firmly apart.*

JOURNALIST. Is Malcolm Tully your real name?

TULLY. It is my name.

JOURNALIST. But not your real name, we can assume?

TULLY. No comment.

JOURNALIST. You are the most wanted terrorist in Britain, are you not?

TULLY. I do not call myself a terrorist. That is their word. They are the terrorists.

JOURNALIST. But you are the most wanted person, are you not?

TULLY. That may be so.

JOURNALIST. And have you personally carried out—what *they* call terrorist activities?

TULLY. I have carried out military operations.

JOURNALIST. And have those operations, as you call them— resulted in—casualties?

TULLY. That is the nature of military operations.

JOURNALIST. Deaths?

TULLY. Ditto.

She looks at him a moment, weightily.

JOURNALIST. And have you actually—pulled the trigger—so to speak?

TULLY *(looking at her legs very deliberately).* I think, looking at your legs, I am getting ideas—so to speak.

JOURNALIST *(sticking to her question).* Have you?

TULLY. No comment.

Scene Eight

The hall. GILDERSLEEVE *is winding up his speech.*

GILDERSLEEVE. Her Majesty's Government, having studied
these conditions, regards them as a basis for detailed
negotiations, and I think—
DUCKER. They are the basis for nothing. They are the
conditions, no more—no less. The only negotiation is about
the implementation of the conditions.

Pause. GILDERSLEEVE *looks down.*

GILDERSLEEVE. That is not my view.
DUCKER. That may not be your view. It is a fact, all the same.
GILDERSLEEVE *(pauses, then restoring his glasses).* Even so, I
am proposing that—
MORAHAN. You are not here to propose, you are here to accept.
If you do not accept, you have wasted our time and your own.
GILDERSLEEVE. Her Majesty's Government have authorized
me to open a wide ranging—
DUCKER. Do you accept the conditions or not?

Blackout and simultaneous spot on TULLY.

TULLY. As we climbed the dark stairs I could hear them
laughing, these boy soldiers, and the girls giggling over that,
like they were starting some sex play. We did not hesitate but
kicked the door back so it smashed back on its hinges,
hitting one of them in the face and scattering their Newcastle
Brown across the floor. It stank of sweat and cigarettes,
soldiers' sweat and soldiers' cigarettes. They were down to their
vests and the girls in bras. The girls got up and grabbed their
pullovers. Not a word. They went straight out. And
immediately the boys went white, white even to the acne on
their skin I noticed. 'Be good lads,' I said, 'take it like men.' But
they were not men, they were whimperers, which caused me to
despise them, and to get it over with I clapped my Browning to
their heads, the barrel in their stubbly skinhead hair, all this
pleading making my fingers shake no end . . .

Full lighting on. GILDERSLEEVE *sits, indicates* AMBER
should lean closer.

GILDERSLEEVE. I am going to have to lose my temper, aren't I?
I don't see what else we can do.
AMBER. Disappointing start, sir.
GILDERSLEEVE. Can't have them walking out, can we?
AMBER. Certainly not.
GILDERSLEEVE. Lose my temper. Carry on from there. *(Pause,
then he stands up and adopts an aggressive posture.)*

The British government is not accustomed to *carte blanche*
acceptance of demands made upon it by unrepresentative
authorities! I came here with a mandate for negotiation and
negotiation is what I am prepared to do. I am not to be shouted
at. I am not a target for your abuse. The door is there. Use it
if you want to. Or let there be some common courtesy. *(He
sits, clears his throat. Pauses.)*
AMBER.   Very good.

Pause.

TULLY *(to* DUCKER).   Tell him thank you for his histrionics.
Then ask him to carry on.

Blackout.

Scene Nine

*The trestle table, the bench, the chairs. Either side, the soldiers
and three terrorist soldiers. They stand, looking at one another for
some time.*

PRIVATE MILLER.   Tell me, Foureyes, why you bastards have to
kill people.
SERGEANT ROYCE.   No talking, Kev.
PRIVATE MILLER.   Asking him a question.
SERGEANT ROYCE.   That's an order.
PRIVATE MILLER.   Simple question! (SERGEANT ROYCE *ignores
him, walks a little way, looks away.)* Why, then? *(No one replies.
They just stare at him.)* Why do you shoot blokes in the back?
SERGEANT ROYCE.   Keep yer voice down.
PRIVATE MILLER.   That's filth, that is. In the back. Real filth.
(Pause.) Tell me, will yer? Because I'm curious. I wanna know
what makes you tick. *(Pause.)* Because I don't think you are human.
I think you are hairy apes.
SERGEANT ROYCE.   Okay, Kevin.
PRIVATE MILLER.   I haven't met one of these bastards and I am
bloody curious! *(He is eyeball to eyeball with one of the
terrorists. Pause.)*
EDEN.   One of your drivers, because he was in a hurry, reversed his
pig truck across my sister. The hairy ape.

Pause.

PRIVATE MILLER.   There is compensation. There is such a thing
as compensation. *(Eden doesn't reply.)* Well, isn't there!
EDEN.   Don't talk. I don't wanna hear your talk.
PRIVATE MILLER.   That is a special case. That is one incident.

EDEN.   One fucking incident. I would shoot you for that one
   fucking incident.
PRIVATE MILLER.   Let me tell you about my mate.
EDEN.   We do not wish to hear about your mate.
PRIVATE MILLER.   Listen.
EDEN.   I won't.
PRIVATE MILLER.   I AM TELLING YOU ABOUT MY MATE!
   (Pause.) This shot . . . this single shot . . . while we were
   talking to some bloody kids . . . this single round from
   nowhere . . . from this prince of snipers . . . from this ace
   gunman . . . this Bisley dream . . . carried half his face
   away . . . and me hiding in a doorway twenty minutes before I
   dared go back to him . . . five yards from me . . . and all these
   people laughing at us . . . face down and very conscious in the
   road . . . *(Pause.)* Then home to Richmond, Surrey . . . this
   plastic thing . . . this prosthesis stuck on his face . . . to this
   place full of old men hideous from World War One . . . my
   mate . . . afraid to pull the curtains . . . drowned himself in the
   park pond . . . through the little hole that used to be his mouth . . .

Long pause.

EDEN.   You want me to be moved. I'm not moved. I am *not*
   moved.

Blackout.

Scene Ten

The hall. GILDERSLEEVE *is talking. Everyone studies street maps
except* TULLY *who watches* GILDERSLEEVE. GLAZING *is standing
by the blackboard with a pointer.*

GILDERSLEEVE.   The proposed area for the first stage of— *(He
   looks up, smiles.)* Disconfrontation—to coin a phrase, I think—
   extends from Albert Terrace—

GLAZING *points, looks puzzled.*

GLAZING.   I think—
GILDERSLEEVE.   No . . . (GLAZING *comes to* GILDERSLEEVE'S
   table. They confer in whispers.) Not Albert Terrace . . . *(He looks up,
   smiles.)* Nelson Street. (GLAZING *returns to the board.)* Nelson
   Street to Canal Buildings. Got that? Okay?
TULLY.   With the passing of the years, could I end up like you, mister?
   When I'm legitimate, will I have your little grins?

Pause. GILDERSLEEVE *looks up, takes his glasses off.*

GILDERSLEEVE.   When I think . . . when I first came to
government . . . how inconceivable this would have been. Us
here. With common murderers . . . *(Pause.)* There was Hitler,
of course. He was a common murderer. *(Pause.)* What a
gorgeous summer that was . . . 1945 . . . after the long week in
Whitehall, going down to the Mill . . . in deckchairs on the
lawn . . . above us . . . going one way—doodlebugs, purring to the
East End . . . high above that, little silver specks . . . our
bombers making for Berlin . . . *(Pause.)* Nothing really shakes us.
Our unstoppable maturity.
TULLY *(taking in* GILDERSLEEVE.)   His suit. A most attractive
suit that is. Cut by London tailors. I have heard Jomo Kenyatta
buys in Saville Row. The badge, that is. Like picking up a crown.
(Pause.) I'm not averse to a decent suit myself. Look at De Valéra.
He had an eye for gear, the old man did. And General Grivas. I
have seen him in a bit of decent cloth. They don't have the
monolopy of good taste.
GILDERSLEEVE *(looking back at* TULLY).   Why are they so
shabby? Is it a sort of uniform I wonder.
TULLY.   I am not to be looked at with that headmaster's look. I
am not a specimen.
GILDERSLEEVE.   The raggedness of phoney populism . . .

Suddenly TULLY *gets up.*

TULLY.   We are soldiers! We don't employ men for our killing so
we can sit in white shirts, mister! *(Pause. He is shaking slightly. The
whole room looks at him.)* So none of your superciliousness, you
nose-wiped people.

Pause, then he sits. GLAZING *is stifling giggles of embarrassment.*
GILDERSLEEVE *stands up.*

GILDERSLEEVE.   I'm afraid I'm not altogether *au fait* with what—
TULLY.   *Au fait* yerself.

MORAHAN *and* DUCKER *laugh.* GILDERSLEEVE *is stung but icy.*

GILDERSLEEVE.   Perhaps I missed something. I rather thought we
were discussing demarcation areas.
TULLY.   Sit down.
GILDERSLEEVE.   I shan't do that.
TULLY.   Oh, sit down!
GILDERSLEEVE.   No, I shan't do that. *(Pause.)* If there is some
matter which you would like—
TULLY.   The matter is, we are not here as some species of wild
dog, mister. If you find us so distasteful, as I sense from your
manner, then fuck off.

GILDERSLEEVE.   Really, I had no idea I was behaving as if in the presence of wild dogs. I can assure you none of us has a muzzle concealed about his person.

GLAZING *roars with laughter.* GILDERSLEEVE *is gratified.*

TULLY *(On his feet).*   Your manner! Your manner is!

Pause, GLAZING *recovers.*

GILDERSLEEVE.   If I may take this opportunity of offering you—a bone—to prolong your metaphor—
TULLY.   Oh, sit down!
GILDERSLEEVE.   I am carrying out these preliminary talks in a manner totally unprejudiced I hope, by any private feelings of distaste.
TULLY.   You are prejudiced.
GILDERSLEEVE.   I do not think so.
TULLY.   You have admitted it.
GILDERSLEEVE.   Not at all.
TULLY.   You have said your private feelings were of distaste.
GILDERSLEEVE.   I have said I am not prejudiced by them.
TULLY.   Well, from here it looks as if you are.
GILDERSLEEVE.   I cannot help the distorted view from your seat.
DUCKER.   I wish you would sit down, mister, you pop up and down too much.
GILDERSLEEVE.   I am not to be spoken to like this.
TULLY.   Please yerself.

GILDERSLEEVE *sits and turns to* AMBER. GLAZING *joins in a mumbled conversation.*

DUCKER *(shouting).*   You sat down, then!
GILDERSLEEVE.   This is a comedy! If you showed it at the pictures, you would not be believed!
GLAZING.   Are we carrying on, sir?
GILDERSLEEVE.   I honestly believe the man is partially insane.
GLAZING.   It's all off then, is it, sir?
GILDERSLEEVE.   Will you not keep saying that!
GLAZING.   I thought perhaps I ought to ring the airport, sir.
GILDERSLEEVE.   I do not want you to ring the airport.
GLAZING.   Sorry, sir.
TULLY *(as they confer).*   I went too far. They are all for going home.
DUCKER.   Good riddance to the turdbrains.
TULLY.   I went too far. They have that manner. They cannot help that manner. They are born with it.
MORAHAN.   They'll stick it out. I was in their army. I know them. They are happy taking stick. It is their schools does it to them.

TULLY. I shall have to patch it.
DUCKER. Don't crawl. Patch it, but don't crawl. *(He looks at
TULLY, warning him.)*
AMBER. I think perhaps it's a device, sir. This throwing of
tantrums. The Reds did the same thing in Korea.
GILDERSLEEVE. Thank you, Amber.
AMBER. The thing is not to sink to their level.
GILDERSLEEVE. All right, Amber, thank you. *(Pause, then he
stands up again, waits for silence.)* I think, if we might carry on,
the Eastward boundary—

TULLY *stands.* GILDERSLEEVE *stops, removes his glasses, waits.*

TULLY. The war of 1939-45. Were you in it? Did you serve?
GILDERSLEEVE. I don't see what bearing that has on the matter.
But yes, I served.
TULLY. A serving soldier, were you? In the forces?
GILDERSLEEVE. For two years. Yes.
TULLY. In battle?
GILDERSLEEVE. Yes.

Pause.

TULLY. Well, for the killing you did, mister, with your hands, I
despise you too. Wild dogs. *(He sits.)*

Pause.

GILDERSLEEVE. For the sake of these discussions I am
prepared to overlook that vile remark. There is nothing
whatsoever in common between what I did as a soldier in the war
against the evil of Nazidom, and what you do and have done.
It is an odious comparison.
AMBER. Hear, hear.
TULLY. I take nothing back. I only ask for you to recognize we are
soldiers, and treat us accordingly.
GILDERSLEEVE. I can only say I have every intention of carrying
through this meeting—
DUCKER. That is not the point. Do you or do you not accord to
us the status of soldiers?
GILDERSLEEVE *(after some thought).* Willingly.
TULLY. Thank you.

Pause.

GILDERSLEEVE. The Eastward boundary of the demarcation area
we now agree will be the Unigate Dairy factory in square—

Blackout.

Scene Eleven

The soldiers and terrorists are sitting now.

FRASER. You have this idea you are decent. That is what I
cannot stand in you.

PRIVATE MILLER. We do what we have to do.

FRASER. But you think you do it decently!

PRIVATE MILLER. Who said I was decent? I have been very
indecent in my time. I feel like being very indecent when I look
at you. Decency goes out the winder when I look at you.

PRIVATE ROSE. If we had behaved like Hitler, this would have
been finished long ago. It's a fact. We would still have had an
empire if we had acted like the *SS*.

SIMS. The pride of these blokes . . . they only lost their
Empire because of their decency . . .

Scene Twelve

*Lights fade on them, fade up on two figures climbing with difficulty
over scaffolding. They are discovered to be* HACKER *and* CLOUT.
HACKER *is pulling* CLOUT *up to the clerestory window.*

HACKER. Christ, Clout . . . do something . . . I'm not . . .
sodding . . . Steve McQueen . . .

CLOUT. Sorry, Mr Hacker . . .

HACKER. Find a footing . . . feel around . . .

CLOUT. Sorry . . . I . . .

HACKER. Christ . . .

CLOUT. Got it. *(He joins* HACKER.)

HACKER *(shaking it)*. My wrist . . . my bloody wrist . . .

CLOUT. Sorry.

HACKER. Keep yer voice down. We're right above 'em here. Move
like a cat. (CLOUT *looks puzzled.)* Sound like a brigade of
fucking guards up here . . . *(He moves carefully along.* CLOUT
drops something with a clatter.) A cat! A bloody CAT! *(They
clamber a little further, peer down to the negotiators below.)*
A sight for sore eyes, Clout. A pow-wow by courtesy of
Hacker Company. Dispositions by Mr Clout . . .

CLOUT. The glass is dirty. Sorry about that.

HACKER. The vital thing is that we did it. Your efforts didn't go
unnoticed. I may say.

CLOUT. Oh . . . *(He shrugs.)*

HACKER. Terrorists may come and terrorists may go, but
conferences will last forever. And the issuing of contracts to the
likes of us. I foresee a time when the refurbishing of the
United Nations will be up for grabs. And I hope to be there.

I hope to be in that league, do you see?

CLOUT *looks at him, mystified. Lights fade on the image of them peering down.*

Scene Thirteen

The hall, still lit. GILDERSLEEVE *is sipping water.*

GILDERSLEEVE. It's our self-assurance niggles him. Gnaws his
prestige. We have this style. This famous style all the great
dictators have remarked upon. He has nothing but his
exhibitionism to pit against our polish and stability . . .

*As they watch each other, a caption is projected on a screen. It
reads,* 'Tully visits the lavatory and has a dream.' *He gets up,
goes out as the light fades on the hall. At the moment of
blackout, a spot on a double bed.*

Scene Fourteen

Sitting in the bed, upright, is the WOMAN JOURNALIST. *Either
side of her, masked, two gunmen. As they stand thus silently, three
rings on a doorbell, very distinctive. A door slams. A second spot
picks out* TULLY, *in an overcoat and holding a bottle of wine or
whisky.*

TULLY *(removing his coat).*   HAVE—YOU—GOT—YOUR
KNICKERS—OFF? *(He laughs, drops the coat down.)* IT'S ME . . .
BIG KNICKER SNIFFER . . . *(He pretends to be a bloodhound
for a few paces. Stops.)* Where are yer? *(Pause.)* I can see you . . .
(He grunts, apelike. She doesn't move a muscle.) What's the
matter?
FRASER.   Get into bed.

TULLY *is paralyzed with horror.*

SIMS.   Fornicator. Into bed. (TULLY *is frozen.)* THE BED. *(He
obeys, not taking his clothes off. He sits beside the* WOMAN
JOURNALIST.)
TULLY.   You've come to murder us.
FRASER.   Our looks speak volumes.
SIMS *(standing back to admire).*   I love that. That sexiness. The
times I have seen her on the telly and thought what sexiness.
TULLY.   Go away, lads, please.
SIMS *(mimicking her voice).*   'And have you actually—pulled the
trigger—so to speak?' So shocked. I did love that.

TULLY. Go on, lads. Before you do something you'll be sorry for.

FRASER. Ask him. If he pulled the trigger.

SIMS. Interview him. Properly. In the bed. Interview the Minister.

TULLY. GO.

FRASER *(mocking him)*. Go. Red Indian chief.

SIMS *(to the* WOMAN JOURNALIST.*)* DO IT!

JOURNALIST. And have you actually—pulled the trigger?

SIMS. SO TO SPEAK!

JOURNALIST. So to speak.

Pause.

SIMS. Did that make your knees knock? And your heart go boompety boom? Did it have you juicing at the thought of it?

FRASER *(to* TULLY*)*. You are so clean now. And once you had sawdust in your hair. And your wardrobe, jammed with SUITS!

SIMS. Suits. One dozen. For the wearing of in parliament.

FRASER. Tailor and Cutter. Best Dressed Public Man award.

TULLY. And are you shooting me for that? You'll be shooting people for the colour of their turds.

SIMS. It's crossed my mind.

Long pause. TULLY *is sweating.*

TULLY. There has been too much murder here! Nothing is resolved by nurder!

SIMS. That's very true. I endorse that sentiment.

TULLY. Assasination is a fantasy. Have you read Lenin on individual terror? *(Pause.)* Have you! Read it! It's downstairs.

SIMS. I have read it. I am not illiterate. And it has made a deep impression on my mind. So much so I have decided you will definitely be the last. *(Pause.)* I promise that.

TULLY *looks at them for some time.*

TULLY. Do it, then. If you've got the bloody nerve. Do it.

JOURNALIST *(trying to pull the sheets over herself.)* No, please, NO!

TULLY. DO IT.

JOURNALIST. SHUT UP! SHUT UP! *(Pause. She screws herself up under the sheet.)* PLEASE!

They watch her, letting the seconds pass.

FRASER. You wouldn't rather it was in the shower, to be there with Danton and the rest?

TULLY. You disgusting bloody house-breaker.

FRASER. Oh, that offends him! Picking his lock! After all the door panes he has shot through, the home is sacred suddenly!

SIMS. You clean man. You Jomo with your fly swat.

FRASER. How you must be wishing for your Do-It-Yourself shop, Malcolm. How you must . . .

TULLY. Shut up and do it.

JOURNALIST. NOT ME! NOT ME!

FRASER. You'll go down in history. Along with Mussolini's tart. She had good legs.

TULLY. DO IT, YOU FILTH!

Pause.

SIMS. All right. Yes.

The lights go out. There is a shot.

Scene Fifteen

The lights on the hall flash on at once, as to the sound of splintering glass, the body of HACKER *falls through the clerestory window and plummets to the floor between the rows of tables. There is instant consternation, shouts off, panic and alarm.*

GILDERSLEEVE. Don't panic! Keep calm! Will you not panic! Everybody sit down, please! *(He shoves* AMBER *back into his chair.)*

GLAZING. Does this mean the talks are cancelled?

GILDERSLEEVE. SIT DOWN!

GLAZING *returns to his place.*

DUCKER. Who is this man?

GILDERSLEEVE. Please, everybody—

DUCKER. This man was an agent—

GILDERSLEEVE. We will wait calmly for a report.

DUCKER. You had a man posted on the roof, is that not correct?

GILDERSLEEVE. I know nothing of this matter. I am as shocked as you. *(He turns to his own ranks.)* WILL SOMEONE FETCH A DOCTOR?

TULLY *(coming in)*. Where are our men? What has happened to our men?

Enter hurriedly SERGEANT ROYCE. *Followed by* EDEN *of the terrorists.*

SERGEANT ROYCE. I'm sorry, sir, I think there's been an accident.

DUCKER. They had an agent on the roof!

Suddenly CLOUT *rushes in, pushing people aside. He rushes to the body of* HACKER *and kneels by it.*

CLOUT. Mr Hacker! Oh, Christ, Mr Hacker . . . oh, Christ . . .

Everyone watches as CLOUT *seems to pull at the corpse, weeping.*

SERGEANT ROYCE. Sir, I was on a routine check of the premises, sir. Every fifteen minutes, sir. Private Miller saw two men on the roof, sir. They did not heed his challenge, sir.

GLAZING. It's Hacker. The contractor, sir.

FRASER *(kneeling by* CLOUT*).* He's dead, I'm no expert but he's dead.

PRIVATE MILLER *appears in the doorway, white.*

DUCKER *(to* TULLY*).* They shoot like cowboys. They are all John Waynes . . .

GILDERSLEEVE. I think he had better be removed. With all respect. He can't stay here. *(He looks to the terrorist delegates.)* I think this only underlines the vast importance of this conference succeeding. It is a solemn warning. Almost a sign from God.

TULLY *(to* DUCKER*).* Always a sentiment for the occasion. If we don't sign today, we'll have God to reckon with. *(He looks at* GILDERSLEEVE.*)* May I suggest we break here, then?

GILDERSLEEVE. Yes, indeed.

TULLY *(to his men).* No cakes.

Two terrorists and two soldiers lift HACKER *away.*

PRIVATE MILLER. I challenged. You heard me challenge, didn't you?

CLOUT. I heard this shout . . .

He begins to drift out. GILDERSLEEVE *stops him.*

GILDERSLEEVE. I wonder, when you've got a minute, if you'd mind—sweeping up this glass? (CLOUT *wanders away.* GILDERSLEEVE *sees* PRIVATE MILLER.) All right?

PRIVATE MILLER. Feel shocking, sir . . .

GILDERSLEEVE. You will do, yes. Bound to for a little while . . . *(He can think of nothing more to say.)* Good . . .

Fade to black.

Scene Sixteen

The body of HACKER *is laid across the trestle table covered with
the Union Jack. Sitting round it,* SERGEANT ROYCE, PRIVATE
ROSE, FRASER, SIMS *and* EDEN. PRIVATE ROSE *is playing
a transistor.* PRIVATE MILLER *appears. He lays down his rifle.
Pause.*

PRIVATE MILLER. Turn that off.
PRIVATE ROSE. Please.
PRIVATE MILLER. If you would. You bastard.
PRIVATE ROSE. Thank you. *(He switches it off.* PRIVATE
  MILLER *sits. Pause).* If this had been the nineteenth century,
  we should have been in any number of exotic places. We
  should have seen a bit of foreign cunt. A few changes of
  kit . . . *(He looks at* PRIVATE MILLER, *who is gazing at
  the body.)* They'll bring a zip-up bag for him.

Pause.

PRIVATE MILLER. I'm not ashamed.
PRIVATE ROSE. Christ, no.
PRIVATE MILLER. If I'd been farting around, then yes, I'd say
  I done wrong. If I was loosing off all round the shop I'd say I
  was wrong. If I was indiscriminate. *(Pause.)* But I did it proper.
  Procedures to the fucking detail. So I've no cause to be ashamed.

Pause, then AMBER *comes in, making his way between the chairs.*

AMBER. Sorry . . . (PRIVATE ROSE *drags his chair forward.*
  AMBER *sees the body.)* Ah. *(Pause.)* I'd no idea . . . you
  see . . . this is an office . . . technically . . .
PRIVATE ROSE. It's a morgue now, squire.
AMBER *(patiently).* I'm not a squire. All right? *(He turns, looks
  at the table.* HACKER *is lying on various papers.)* There are
  some papers here . . . (HACKER *is immovable.)* I do think,
  whoever brought him here . . .
PRIVATE ROSE. We did.
AMBER. Yes. Well, there are some papers here. *(He tries to pull
  at them.)* You've laid him on our papers.
PRIVATE MILLER. Just leave him. Don't fiddle with him.
AMBER. You'll have to lift him, I'm afraid.
PRIVATE MILLER. LEAVE HIM!

Pause. AMBER *looks about him.*

AMBER. You are being melodramatic.
PRIVATE MILLER. I will be melodramatic. I will smack you on the
  nose.

AMBER *gives him a contemptuous look, then goes out.* FRASER
looks out after him.

FRASER. There's tea out here. *(He gets up. To* PRIVATE MILLER.)
I'm not bringing it for yer, but there's tea out here.

Scene Seventeen

The hall. Both groups drink tea, drifting round their seperate ends.
AMBER *appears.*

GILDERSLEEVE *(looking at the full pastry trays).*   Not a bit.
Not one of them has taken a bite.
AMBER.   I wasn't able to get all the lists. They have put the
contractor's body on our papers and are guarding it like starved
alsatians
GILDERSLEEVE.   It's not important.
AMBER.   They have put him on top of the statistics.
GILDERSLEEVE.   Please. (AMBER *sighs.)* Have you noticed . . .
how they haven't eaten anything?

Scene Eighteen

The soldiers are standing round the body drinking tea. SERGEANT
ROYCE *sees the* CATERERS *pass by with full trays.*

SERGEANT ROYCE.   Oi, Mrs, where you going with them cakes?
CATERER.   Home.
SERGEANT ROYCE.   Home? You can't eat that lot, can yer?
CATERER.   Got em for the old man's tea. They don't want em.
I'm not wasting 'em.
SERGEANT ROYCE. Pass 'em over here, then.

She comes in. The soldiers help themselves.

1ST CATERER.   Must have thought they were poisoned. Thought
there was drugs in 'em.
PRIVATE ROSE.   I fancy a trip. What is it, LSD?
SERGEANT ROYCE.   Cannabis doughnut please, darling.
1ST CATERER *(looking at* HACKER'S *body).*   Is that him?
SERGEANT ROYCE.   That's him. He should be in a bag except
we haven't got one.
1ST CATERER.   Who was it that did it?
PRIVATE MILLER.   Me.
1ST CATERER.   I feel more sorry for you than I do for him.
PRIVATE MILLER.   Cheers.

1ST CATERER.   Never leave you, I expect.
PRIVATE ROSE.   Charming.
1ST CATERER.   Conscience is a funny thing. *(She looks at them.)* You lot have the cakes between you. You deserve it. You have a rotten job, you lot. *(She goes out, leaving the tray.)*
SERGEANT ROYCE.   We should start a whip-round. All this bloody sympathy.

PRIVATE ROSE *is about to plunge into a second cake.*

PRIVATE ROSE.   What about them?
SERGEANT ROYCE.   Who?
PRIVATE ROSE *(indicating the terrorists).*   THEM.
SERGEANT ROYCE *(with a shrug).*   Ask 'em.
PRIVATE ROSE *(holding out a doughnut).*   Doughnut? (EDEN *shakes his head.)* NO? *(He picks another.)* Arsenic slice?

They all laugh. Blackout.

Scene Nineteen

The hall. The tea and the cakes have gone. The negotiators are at their tables. All are sitting but for TULLY. *Pause.*

TULLY.   I am not going to make a speech. But I am taking this opportunity before resumption of negotiations to refresh your memories on certain matters which may be weighing heavily on you. Such as the notion that this ceasefire is a vital matter to us, which it is not. We can continue our campaign on any level, whatever the cost. We are not here as suers for peace. I hope that's clear.
GILDERSLEEVE.   Methinks he doth protest too much . . .
TULLY.   And secondly, to emphasize we sit here as your equals, and that your centuries of diplomatic practice cut no ice with us. We are not after becoming constitutional animals, domesticated by the British government, learning Westminster at your tit. It is on the line what we are here for. Not to be terrorized. Not to be driven into concentration camps—
GILDERSLEEVE *(rising quickly to his feet).*   I am sorry. This is what is called a speech.
TULLY.   The invention of which—
GILDERSLEEVE.   If this is not a speech, will someone tell me what is—
TULLY.   The invention of which the British must take credit for.
GILDERSLEEVE.   You really must not exploit every opportunity of making propoganda like this—

TULLY.   During the Boer War. I have it on authority.

GILDERSLEEVE.   We will stick to the agenda.

TULLY.   The British introduced the concentration camp in 1900. For women and children. It is a fact.

GILDERSLEEVE.   We will stick to the agenda! *(Pause. TULLY sits.)* Thank you for the speech you assured us you would not make. *(Low laughter from* GLAZING.*)* Now if we might move on to point two of the agenda. The status of convicted criminals.

DUCKER.   CRIMINALS!

GILDERSLEEVE.   Criminals, yes. It is our policy that—

DUCKER.   CRIMINALS? (GILDERSLEEVE *stops, removes his glasses, looks at* DUCKER.) That word.

GILDERSLEEVE.   Yes?

DUCKER.   THAT WORD.

GILDERSLEEVE.   Well, I have no intention of changing it.

DUCKER.   We cannot talk about criminals. There is no conversation to be had about criminals.

GILDERSLEEVE.   The word is our word. For men who have been convicted by due process of law. You have your interpretation, we have ours.

DUCKER.   It is not a word. It is a downright lie.

Pause.

GILDERSLEEVE.   I am not a liar.

DUCKER.   Your vocabulary has bad habits, then.

Pause GILDERSLEEVE *sits, murmurs with* AMBER.

TULLY.   Give him his word.

DUCKER.   Give him his word! His word is an insult to the men who suffer from it!

DUCKER *glares at* TULLY. *Pause.* TULLY *stands.*

TULLY.   Can we agree to call them prisoners?

Pause.

GILDERSLEEVE.   This is our man . . . *(He stands.)* The word is not in dispute as I understand it. It is a matter of interpretation. It is a matter of describing the condition of having been convicted for offences of a civil nature before the British courts—

TULLY.   Do we have to be so lawyerish? I am all for plain English.

Pause.

GILDERSLEEVE.   Me too. *(He smiles.)*

Pause.

DUCKER *(looking from* GILDERSLEEVE *to* TULLY). You English.
   You are all so English . . .
AMBER. Should I get a dictionary?

Pause. GILDERSLEEVE *is gazing at* TULLY. *At last he breaks.*

GILDERSLEEVE. No. the word's the word. I'm sticking there.

AMBER *is shocked by* GILDERSLEEVE's *attitude.* TULLY
disappointed. GILDERSLEEVE *sits.*

TULLY *(to* DUCKER). We're losing time. While we quibble over
   words our people are being beaten in their gaols. They would not
   be over-concerned about a word.
DUCKER. Ever since we came here we have used their words. This
   is the flag all over again. Their words are their secret weapons. We
   have to fight their language too.

Pause.

TULLY. No. We must go on. *(He addresses* GILDERSLEEVE.)
   This word . . . if we do not say the word . . . if we refrain from
   it, so when we come to use it, we say . . . *(He shrugs.)*
GILDERSLEEVE *(helpfully).* Buzz?

Muffled sniggers from GLAZING. GILDERSLEEVE *knows he has
secured a coup.*

TULLY. What you like.
GILDERSLEEVE *(to himself).* We have found him. We have
   found our treasure. *(Pause, then to them.)* As I was indicating—
DUCKER *(petulantly).* SAYING!
GILDERSLEEVE *(patiently).* There can be no possibility of an
   immediate change of status for those— *(he stops, smiles)*
   Buzzes—that we hold in custody at least until we have firm
   evidence—

Blackout.

Scene Twenty

The soldiers and the terrorists are eating with a will.

PRIVATE ROSE. I'm gonna be sick. Like the Romans at an orgy.
   Stuff, puke and stuff again.
FRASER. Don't they feed you properly? You starving bastards.
SERGEANT ROYCE. I have never witnessed such an exhibition of
   downright greed. *(He grabs another slice.)*

SIMS. If he gets shot, he starts leaking artificial cream . . .

They laugh, mouths overflowing.

PRIVATE ROSE. I'm gonna be shot, am I? *(He looks at the terrorists.)* Am I? You reckon?

PRIVATE MILLER. Go on. Tell him if he will be shot.

EDEN. He has a fair chance, I would say.

PRIVATE MILLER *(to* PRIVATE ROSE). You heard the man.

PRIVATE ROSE. Not after today. Not after the signatures are on
  the bits of paper. Home, then. Home to my mum and the fat tart
  who has been writing with such unnatural regularity.

EDEN. We hope so, yes. You are doing no good here.

SERGEANT ROYCE. This here— *(He indicates* HACKER'S
  body.) This here could be the final casualty. A civilian, we
  note.

PRIVATE MILLER *(to* EDEN). I would rather it had been one
  of you. Frankly.

SIMS. Likewise, of course.

PRIVATE MILLER. Nothing could water down my hatred for
  this place.

FRASER. You should not have come here.

PRIVATE MILLER. That's not my concern, mate! That's not a
  soldier's business, where he should and should not go.

EDEN. Then I feel sorry for you.

PRIVATE ROSE. Oh, not another one.

SERGEANT ROYCE. You reckon it's been worth it, do you? If
  you get what you want from this?

SIMS. Yes.

SERGEANT ROYCE *(nodding towards* HACKER). With him
  there . . . and the others . . .

SIMS. Yes.

SERGEANT ROYCE. Fanaticism, that is. If you want my
  opinion.

PRIVATE MILLER. Mad dogs.

EDEN. Tomorrow, they tell you—go and kill a Chinaman. On
  Friday, go and kill an African. On Saturday, a Jap. I call that mad.
  Mad dogs bite anyone.

PRIVATE MILLER. Mickey, reel off our battle honours.

PRIVATE ROSE. I'm eating.

PRIVATE MILLER. Tell him.

PRIVATE ROSE *(wiping his mouth, reciting like a poem).*
  Inkerman, Lucknow, Kabul, Accra, Peking, Tel-el-Kebir,
  Majuba Hill, Ladysmith, First Ypres, the Somme, Cambrai,
  Mesopotamia, Dunkirk, El Alamein, Cyprus, Kenya, Borneo.
  (He stops, licks his fingers, eats on.)

PRIVATE MILLER.   The purity of that. Against all your bleeding faith.

Scene Twenty-one

The hall. GILDERSLEEVE *is sitting now.* AMBER *is talking.*

TULLY.   Our position on this is fundamental. Political status for prisoners is the condition of the ceasefire.
DUCKER.   No room for manoeuvre!

Pause.

AMBER.   As you know, it is not possible for us to—
DUCKER.   No point in going on!

Pause.

AMBER.   We have achieved a measure of agreement on other issues where it did not originally appear—
TULLY.   This is different.
AMBER.   I don't see why it—
TULLY.   This is fundamental.

AMBER *is beginning to lose confidence.* GILDERSLEEVE *will not even assist him with a glance.*

AMBER.   All right, but can't we—
TULLY.   It's yes or no.

Pause. AMBER *is stuck for a response.*

AMBER.   I cannot agree that it's a question of yes or no—
TULLY.   It is.
AMBER.   No, no, it isn't . . .
TULLY.   I say it is.
AMBER.   No, no . . .

DUCKER *lets out a groan.* GILDERSLEEVE *gets up, looks at* AMBER.

GILDERSLEEVE.   Carry on in that vein, will you? For a minute?

AMBER *looks horrified as* GILDERSLEEVE *deserts him for the lavatory. He takes a sip of water. Blackout.*

Scene Twenty-two

The soldiers and the body. They are smoking.

PRIVATE MILLER.   I am an Arnheim orphan. We die in useless

campaigns. My grandad died in Flanders. I have toured both
districts. They are nothing districts, but beautiful in comparison
with this.

GILDERSLEEVE *comes in. He looks at them. They look back. He
goes through to the lavatory.*

EDEN. All military campaigns that are not revolutionary are
useless.
PRIVATE MILLER. Is that a fact?
EDEN. It is a fact.
SIMS. He's a left-winger, aren't you son?
EDEN. The English army has not fought a revolutionary war
since the seventeenth century.
PRIVATE MILLER. I wouldn't know.
EDEN. It is a fact. All their lost blood is useless blood, spilled in
oppression. The world is spotted with their useless blood . . .

They look at him. Sound of unsuccessful flushing of a lavatory.
GILDERSLEEVE *reappears. Pause.*

GILDERSLEEVE. I wonder if . . . should you be all together like this,
do you think? *(They look puzzled.)* Quite honestly? Do you think?
SERGEANT ROYCE *(standing, brushing himself down).*   Not if
you don't think so, sir—
PRIVATE MILLER. WHY NOT. (GILDERSLEEVE *looks shocked,*
SERGEANT ROYCE *embarrassed.)* Whassit matter?
SERGEANT ROYCE. You heard.
PRIVATE MILLER. They're having talks. Up there. They are
sitting with the enemy. And I am sitting with these geezers. I am
having talks. Our talks.
SERGEANT ROYCE. GET ON YOUR FEET!

Pause. GILDERSLEEVE *waits.*

PRIVATE MILLER. I am guarding this body. I am not moving.

Pause, then GILDERSLEEVE *goes out. Fade to black.*

Scene Twenty-Three

The hall. AMBER *is on his feet, but silent.* GILDERSLEEVE, *taut
with anger, comes in, takes his place*

GILDERSLEEVE. What's happening?
AMBER. There appears to be a deadlock, I thought—
GILDERSLEEVE. I told you to keep talking.
AMBER. Well, I did, but—
GILDERSLEEVE. Keep talking, then.
AMBER. What—just—

GILDERSLEEVE. TALK.

Pause, then with desperate embarrassment, AMBER *forces himself on.*

AMBER.   I think you're probably—quite clear—about our point of view—if I could only—
DUCKER.   You are clear and we are clear.

AMBER *looks desperately to* GILDERSLEEVE, *who gazes round the room.*

AMBER.   All the same, for clarification—
TULLY.   We are not here for the pleasure of your accent. If you have something new to say, then say it.
AMBER.   Yes . . . *(Pause.)* Well, yes . . . nevertheless, there seems no harm in making absolutely certain that . . . *(He just dries.)*
DUCKER *(shaking his head).*   Jesus Christ . . .

Pause. GILDERSLEEVE *makes a slight gesture with his finger for* AMBER *to sit, and he does so with relief. Pause, then* GILDERSLEEVE *stands.*

GILDERSLEEVE.   This is dragging on. It is not of such importance we can tolerate it dragging on. *(Pause.)* I want to be in London within the hour. *(He sits.)*

There are gasps from the terrorists, a smile from GLAZING.

TULLY.   Well, that . . . that leaves me speechless . . .
DUCKER *(on his feet).*   That is a monstrous tactic! That is a blatant attempt to bulldoze this delegation!
TULLY.   You'll have to withdraw that statement. There is no question of negotiating under threat.
DUCKER.   My God, man, my God.

Pause.

GILDERSLEEVE.   Nevertheless, it stands. *(He removes his watch, lays it in front of him.)*
TULLY.   Five hundred years of English diplomacy . . .
DUCKER.   We go. We pack up and go. *(He starts gathering his papers up.)*
TULLY.   Hold it.
DUCKER.   We go, don't we?
TULLY.   Not yet.
DUCKER.   He has his bloody watch in front of him!
TULLY.   I can see him.
DUCKER.   We are not his bloody schoolboys.
TULLY.   Will you sit still.

They look at each other. Pause.

DUCKER.   Christ, I think you are going to give in to him . . .

Pause.

TULLY.   We have done good work today. A good deal has been
   done, in a spirit of reasonable compromise. I think this is endangered
   by the statement you have made. I urge you to retract it.

Pause.

GILDERSLEEVE.   We're wasting time.

TULLY.   I urge you.

GILDERSLEEVE.   You have our offer.

Pause. TULLY *sits.* AMBER *leans over to* GILDERSLEEVE.

AMBER.   Don't you think . . . *(He shifts uncomfortably.)* I do
   think we . . . we don't seem to be allowing much room for
   manoeuvre . . . de we? *(Pause.)* Or do we?

GILDERSLEEVE *ignores him.*

DUCKER.   Get up. And go. Walk to the door. *(Pause.)*
   Christ, man!

TULLY.   If we go, that's the finish. We get nothing if we go.

DUCKER.   We are not here as beggars. Let's go!

TULLY.   You have no politics in you.

DUCKER.   I have none!

TULLY.   Change comes about through small gains, which are then
   exploited. Get your finger in the door, then prise it open. Don't
   charge it with your head. *(Pause.)* I'm after an agreement.

DUCKER.   On his terms.

TULLY.   I have spat the pride out. I find it only when I need it,
   as a tactic. For its own sake, pride is a burden. *(Pause. He stands
   up.)* We came here in good faith, and you have put the entire
   meeting at risk by your intransigence. But we are not going to be
   provoked. You have come here like Hitler at the Berchtesgarten,
   but we will not let that—

GILDERSLEEVE *(spotting his opportunity).*   That is unacceptable!
   I demand you withdraw that statement!

DUCKER.   FAIR COMMENT!

GILDERSLEEVE.   Withdraw that statement!

DUCKER.   ⎫
         ⎬ NEVER! NEVER!
MORAHAN. ⎭

TULLY *is trapped. He looks at his own side. Their resolution is
obvious.*

GILDERSLEEVE.   You have twice imputed Nazi methods or
   sympathies to me. It is no way to carry on a conference. You will
   withdraw the statement.

DUCKER.   He will NOT!

Pause. GILDERSLEEVE *stands.*

GILDERSLEEVE. How dare you, with the stench of your rotten
crimes hanging about you . . . and your murders and your
maimings . . . how dare you . . .

He shudders slightly. Pause, then DUCKER *grabs up his papers and
followed by* MORAHAN, *walks out.* AMBER *watches, riveted.
Only* TULLY *remains. He gathers his things.*

TULLY. You've thrown it away. It won't come as easy another
time.

Blackout.

Scene Twenty-four

The soldiers are sitting idly. SIMS *enters.*

SIMS. It's all over.
PRIVATE ROSE. Home James! Peace in our time!
SIMS. Hold it . . .
PRIVATE ROSE. Look out Catterick, here we come! *(He jumps up.)*
SIMS. Hold it. There is no agreement.

Pause.

PRIVATE ROSE. Christ, what do they do in there!

Pause, then the terrorists collect up their weapons. PRIVATE ROSE
looks distraut.

PRIVATE MILLER They make monkeys out of us. *(Pause.)*
But us, not such big monkeys, because we have no hopes to be
shat on.
PRIVATE ROSE. I have! I have been here years and not been shot.
I have hopes.

They struggle into their equipment. FRASER *and* SIMS *go out.*
EDEN *hangs back, looks at* PRIVATE MILLER.

EDEN. Stay behind your tin shutters . . . you marksman, you.

He goes out. Enter GLAZING *and* AMBER *to collect their coats.*

GLAZING *(studying his watch).* I'm going to make the stock cars.
There for flag-up with a bit to spare. What's the flying time to
Heathrow?
AMBER. Thirty minutes.
GLAZING. Time to ring one of the ladies. *(He looks at* PRIVATE
MILLER.)* Can you ring London direct from here? (PRIVATE
MILLER *ignores him.)* Charming fellow. Did I see a phone down
there?

AMBER. Yes.

GLAZING. Right. *(He grabs up two official bags, then for the first time notices* HACKER.*)* Christ, is that him? *(He looks at* PRIVATE MILLER.*)* Can I take a butchers? Just a peep? *(*PRIVATE MILLER *ignores him. He lifts the corner of the flag. Pause. He lets it go.)* When he put that tender in, he never thought . . . *(Pause.)* Moral. Never submit a low tender.

He goes out, followed by AMBER.

Scene Twenty-five

The hall. GILDERSLEEVE *is wandering round in coat and hat. The tables are being taken away by the* REMOVAL MEN. AMBER *comes in, stands watching him. Pause.*

AMBER. Do you mind if I'm honest? *(Pause.)* I must say this. I'm sorry. But I think you are a liability. (GILDERSLEEVE *does not respond, still stares up at the clerestory.)* Well, I've said it. I feel very bitter and I had to say something. I'd rather say it to you than go behind your back.

Pause.

GILDERSLEEVE. You shouldn't have. You have done yourself irreparable harm.

AMBER. Yes. I wanted to be frank.

GILDERSLEEVE. You have been. *(Pause.* AMBER *turns to go.)* I had instructions. These talks were never taken seriously. (AMBER *looks shocked.)* Find out the compromisers. That's all we had to do.

Pause. AMBER *looks crestfallen. He goes out. The* REMOVAL MEN *carry out the last chair and table.* GILDERSLEEVE *pulls on his gloves, goes out. The hall is empty. After a few moments,* CLOUT *appears. He goes, stands beneath the clerestory, then kneels. He writes on the floor with a piece of chalk.* SERGEANT ROYCE *comes in, dangling keys.*

SERGEANT ROYCE. Locking up, old son. (CLOUT *works on, ignoring him.* SERGEANT ROYCE *walks into the hall, gazing around.)* I am an unlucky bleeder. In terms of History. Some other bleeder will have guard duty at the next one, the one that matters, the one that goes down in the books. Some bastard from the Fusiliers. *(He looks at* CLOUT.*)* Locking up. *(He jangles the keys.)*

CLOUT. Hang on.

SERGEANT ROYCE *stands over him, reading the chalked message.*

SERGEANT ROYCE.   Like Nelson on the Victory . . .

CLOUT *finishes, stands up, looks at it.*

CLOUT.   On this spot A. Hacker died, during the peace talks, 1975.

SERGEANT ROYCE *(walking to the door).*   By the time this hole
is opened up again, the rats will have rubbed it off with their
little tiny feet . . . *(He holds the door open.)* COME ON!

Blackout.

THE END